THE ROAD TO Chatto Creek

THE ROAD TO Chatto Creek

Leaving the rat race for life in the country

MATT CHISHOLM

Photography by Lottie Hedley

ALLEN&UNWIN
AUCKLAND • SYDNEY • MELBOURNE • LONDON

To family and friends
who give me their time

For me, there's not a whole lot more annoying than the saying: 'If you've got 5 acres, you might as well have 5,000.' If I had a dollar for every time I've heard that, I'd probably be able to buy the 5,000 acres — but obviously I'm not getting a dollar every time I hear that saying. And the reason the saying pisses me off so much is that I can't afford the 5,000 acres. Sure, I get the point of the saying — but you can't just tell me something. I've got to figure it out for myself.

CONTENTS

INTRODUCTION

Summer in Central Otago. I don't believe in perfection, anymore, but it was almost perfect. After another full-on year we could take the foot off the accelerator, slow down and enjoy it. And 'it' was almost everything we'd ever wanted; our dream. It felt like we were staying in a palatial new holiday home, on a stunning bit of dirt in one of the most beautiful places on the planet — Chatto Creek. It didn't feel like ours; didn't feel like we deserved it. But this wasn't temporary. This wasn't a reasonably priced B&B we were sharing with two or three other families for a week over the festive period. *This was our new home.* And while it wasn't in the South Island's tourist Mecca — nearby Queenstown or Wānaka — for me it was equally as beautiful and a whole lot more fitting. It was heartland New Zealand. Where people can't afford to be pretentious. Where they'd give you the shirt off their back. It was beautiful. Quiet. Peaceful. Real. From our oversized macrocarpa dining table we could look south over mousey-brown, arid hills and rocky outcrops, down to Alexandra. To the north we could see the Dunstan Mountains and sun-kissed hills that could have been painted by local artist Grahame Sydney. It was an amazing place to simply be. After a reasonably chaotic life, I reckon I came here to cruise.

It was the summer holiday season, but we weren't going anywhere. Even if we could have afforded to go away, we would've stayed home. Elle and I, along with our three young kids — Bede (six), Finn (four) and Bree (one) — had found our piece of paradise, built our forever home, and wanted to spend as much time as possible on 'The Land' and in that new house. Well, at least I did. My paid work might have been on ice over the silly season, but I still had heaps to do and I'd been looking forward to doing it for ages. Farming was an obsession of mine; an obsession that had consumed a large chunk of my overactive, obsession-prone mind for decades — and I was finally having a crack at it, albeit on a very small scale. I had a real spring in my step.

Farming was an obsession of mine; an obsession that had consumed a large chunk of my overactive, obsession-prone mind for decades — and I was finally having a crack at it.

I had just finished weaning my 80 lambs from their mothers, and they were looking great. But there was a small problem. I had to get those freshly weaned lambs back in to 'the yards' the day after weaning them off their mothers, because I still needed to crutch, vaccinate and drench them. I'd run out of time the day before. It was a situation that experienced and efficient farmers wouldn't find themselves in. And it nearly broke me.

Being mid-January, it was hot. Maybe mid-20s. I let our old dog, Shade, out of the garage and cranked up the Barry Crump-like Toyota Hilux ute. Ten-year-old Shade, a beautiful brown-and-tan huntaway, instantly knew the job was on and started bouncing around and barking like a pup. As usual, though, his enthusiasm was short-lived. It turns out that getting newly weaned lambs back in to the yards is something you're not supposed to do. Those lambs were in a paddock right beside their mothers, which is apparently another thing you're not supposed to do. Well, they *should* all have been in a paddock right beside their mothers, but as soon as I put them in that paddock I watched half a dozen go under the gate to be back with their mothers.

The remaining lambs, those that were still actually weaned, look like they're lining up for the dole in South Dunedin. Seventy-odd lambs, in a line, single file. 'Maaahhhh maaahhhh.' Hard up against the fence next to their bleating mums. I send Shade around behind them: 'Get away back.' We reckon Shade's had a stroke, so he's only good for about five minutes until I have to carry the old bugger. He still barks, though. 'Rohhh rohhh rohhh.' Scared of the dog, the lambs head up the hill, away from the fence and their mothers for about 10–15 metres, before cutting back to beeline it for their mums. I send Shade back twice, but the same thing happens. Twice. After just three failed attempts to get those freshly weaned lambs away from the fence and their mothers for good, Shade's cooked, and is now lying in the stinking-hot Central Otago sun, tongue out, as dry as an old chip, panting away like a young sea lion on heat. Still barking when he can, 'Roohhhh rooohhh rohhh', he's more of a hindrance than a help.

Now it's down to just me and a red 1999 Toyota Hilux ute that I paid about $10,000 too much for because, coming out of Auckland, I thought it was really cool. And whether I'm behind the wheel in the cab, or on my feet chasing those sheep like an overweight schoolboy, I must've gone around those bloody lambs about a hundred times before I finally get them off that fence and away from their mothers for good. They won't shut up, either. 'Maahhhhh mahhhhh mahhhh.' It is almost like they know my name and are taunting me. 'Maaatttt maaattttt maaattttt . . . You haven't beaten us yet, Matttt . . . You're losing, Maaaatttt.'

By now I'm really really steaming, and I guess one of the reasons why I'm really really steaming is because I'm not doing this farming for the money, I'm doing it as a hobby. I'm doing it because it's my passion; I'm doing it for love. Farming is meant to make me feel good when I don't feel good, and I often don't feel good. It's meant to be my medicine.

I still have plenty to do to get those lambs to my father-in-law's yards, and in doing it I break my unwritten rule and drive over the 'k-line' (aka

fancy irrigation system) and rip it out of the hydrant. With water spurting about 20 metres up into the air, the Otago Central Rail Trailers now have something else to look at other than those stunning Grahame Sydney-like hills. And that's not the worst thing. As I shut off the valve to stem the flow of that precious, much-talked-about Manuherikia Valley water, I spot 'The Land 268' — the stud Southdown ewe lamb with a broken leg that's already cost me about 400 bucks in vet bills. It reminds me to ring the vet.

'G'day, mate, Matt Chisholm here from Chatto Creek.'

'Yeah, I know who it is, Cowboy,' he replies.

I ask, 'Is it time to check the lamb, recast her, spend another 200 bucks I'll never get back?'

While I'm on the phone, jinking and jiving in the old ute, trying to stop the freshly weaned lambs from cutting back down the hill to their mothers one more time, I hear this very loud and menacing 'Dink . . . Dink'.

With worry in my voice, I end the conversation with the vet. 'Shit, mate, I'll ring you next week — I think I've just run over a couple of lambs.'

And I had. Taking their sweet time, two lambs hobble out from under the ute. One lies down, frothing from her mouth, and doesn't move for the next hour.

IF I WERE TO WRITE a list of all the many things I love, animals — as much as they can frustrate me at times — would be right up there near the top of the list. And, weirdly, sheep would be right up there near the top of my 'most loved animals' list. And . . . I've just run over two sheep. I feel terrible. Small-scale farming — the gig I'd recently changed my entire life for, the thing that's meant to bring me so much joy — is crushing me. The conversation I'm now having with myself is awful. In that moment, I think about ending my life — again.

Then I remember: I've been here before, and I've been here before often. *I know how to deal with the situation.* My wife's not with me but I can hear her voice in my ear, giving me advice. I do my breathing exercises. Breathe in through my nose and hold for four seconds. Breathe out through my mouth and hold for four seconds. I tell myself I'm a good person. That I'm making some kind of contribution to the world. I tell myself that I'm not losing, I'm learning.

I eventually snap out of it, and crack on. Yard all the lambs, including the two I'd run over; thankfully they both appear to be okay. I rip in to the vaccinating and drenching in my father-in-law's poorly set up semi-permanent sheep yards — my fault, not his — laboriously handling every single lamb, one after the other, as the hours tick by.

I do a lot of public speaking nowadays, and when I tell this story I usually say that my father-in-law, Dennis — a red-blooded man's man nicknamed 'Fizzer' — drives past in his big red Case tractor. And I usually say that Fizzer looks down on me from 3 metres up, from the cab of his Case, and mutters, 'Look at this bloody idiot. I can't believe my beautiful baby daughter married this muppet.' Now, of course I didn't actually hear Dennis saying that, but sometimes the look he gives me when I'm battling away in his yards makes me think he says it often. And of course it hurts, but I'm determined and I continue battling away, 'living my dream' with my sheep, and I eventually finish the job. A one-hour job that has taken me most of the day.

When I get home and put the left-over vaccine in the garage fridge, I notice that it's not that cold in there, and then I notice that someone has turned the fridge off at the wall and I don't know how long it's been off. So: I spent all day gearing up to vaccinate and then vaccinating my lambs with a vaccine that will probably no longer work. When I eventually communicate with some experts, on Facebook, I confirm what I already know — I'll have to do all that work again tomorrow.

Living your dream down on the farm can be delightful, but at times that dream can also be a bloody nightmare.

Classic

IT'S IN THE BLOOD

I've always been mad keen on farming. Right from a really young age, I'd always wanted to live on some land and farm a few animals. No matter what happened in life, I planned to end up on 50 acres. No matter how I was bringing home the bacon, I never once took my eyes off that prize.

Being born half an hour south of Dunedin in Milton, South Otago, it's probably not that surprising. Milton, which is a little farming and forestry town, more than likely got its name from the woollen mills that were once among Otago's largest factories. My old man, Alan, was a stock agent and part-time farmer there in the 1970s and '80s. Some of my earliest memories are of heading out with him as he visited his farmer clients and drafted sheep and cattle for sales or for the freezing works. I was probably dropped off at home before he'd done his day's work because I asked too many questions. Once home, I'd give my mum, Joss, a report on where we'd been and what we'd done — whether she wanted to know or not. 'We went to McElrea's and drafted off 450 mixed-sex lambs for Burnside. Dad reckons they'll make about 35 bucks.' Mum (who was a hairdresser) would have been busy cutting hair, cooking dinner, or baking cakes and biscuits destined initially for the brown-and-orange Tupperware and eventually for our lunches. Mum would've been really busy, but she would've listened.

We lived in a nice new home, on a couple of acres beside the primary school, but for a few years Dad also leased about 500 acres near Toko Mouth. He ran about 1,000 Perendale ewes and would put a Shorthorn bull over about 35 Hereford-cross cows every year. In spring there were pet lambs to feed. I've always loved feeding pet lambs. I'd try to stay up all night just to make sure a wee lamb would live. When I brought in the often wet or frosty *Otago Daily Times*, I'd go straight to the 'Livestock, Birds and Poultry' section. (Forty years on and I'm still doing the same thing, but now on Trade Me.) I'd be at every A&P Show or poultry expo I could get to. Sometimes I'd head down to the Balclutha sale with Dad and 'buy' sheep or cattle I didn't know I'd bid on. Occasionally I'd travel down there and back in a big stock truck, which was always cooler than going by car even though the old Kingswoods and Falcons were pretty bloody cool. When you're seven, it's hard to top cruising to Clutha with the man-mountain Otago rugby lock Dick Knight in a big old Kenworth truck.

It didn't matter whether I was inside or outside, at home or down at the farm, I was either playing sport or I was 'farming'. If Dad had something to do down at our lease block, 'Sunnyvale', I was with him — mustering, marking, shearing, drafting, weaning, killing or butchering animals. And if Dad didn't have anything to do down at Sunnyvale and it was a good day, I was at home, 'farming'. There were always chickens, pigs, calves and dogs to feed and water. Sometimes there were eggs to collect and sheep to move. Even if there weren't any jobs to do, on a good day at least I would be out in our wee paddocks mucking around. I bought half a dozen sheep of my own when I was about eight years old. Despite being average sheep, they had big numbered tags in their ears so I could monitor their progress from one year to the next. Even as a young boy I was behaving like a stud breeder, just with normal sheep. And those sheep produced a valuable fleece of wool every eight months and dropped lambs every year, which always meant I had heaps of money for ice-blocks and lollies on our summer holidays camping in Wānaka. When I was a kid, farming seemed easy.

We always had dogs, and Dad must've bought a new pup about the same time I was born. I'm pretty sure I grew up with 'Rock', a beautiful black-and-tan huntaway who was not only brilliant with sheep and cattle but also a really good mate. He was such a special, gentle creature. Us kids always wanted to give him extra perks, like letting him inside and feeding him what we were having for dinner, but Dad was always quick to remind us, 'Rock's a bloody working dog — get him outside.' As soon as school was finished, and when there wasn't a sports practice or game on, I'd head straight home, grab some tucker and go and let Rock off his leash. I'd send him around my sheep, trying to work him just as Dad did on a much bigger mob. 'Get away out Rock . . . Stand . . . Stand . . . Speak up.' Those poor sheep would head in and out of the yards 50 times a week. It wasn't a complete waste of time, though. While the sheep were in the yards, I'd auction them, just as Dad did down at Clutha or in Dunedin, at Burnside. Usually I was the only person at the auction. But it didn't matter. On the land with those animals was easily my happy place. I can't remember what it was about it exactly, but I just loved it. I remember, more than once, my parents encouraging me to go and do normal kid stuff, like ride bikes and skateboards or swim in the local pool, and I did do all that stuff — occasionally — but I'd normally just hang out on the land with those animals, usually by myself. If it hadn't been for Mum yelling, 'Dinner . . . Dean . . . Aaron . . . Nick . . . Matthew — it's dinner, tea's ready', I'd probably still be out in that back paddock in Milton now.

Growing up in the country there were always jobs to do, and my brothers and I were brought up to work, to roll our sleeves up and muck in. But as the youngest of four boys by three and a half years, my older brothers always seemed more practical, more physically competent, than me. So when the job was on, I probably did more watching and talking than anything else. I soon became the funny guy, the morale officer, which meant I probably ended up doing even less physical work. On top of that, I'm pretty sure that when mistakes were made or work wasn't up to scratch, we soon found out about it. Naturally, I started to climb in to

activities that suited me better. I still made a contribution but, rightly or wrongly, I started to question my physical abilities. I started telling myself that, at least practically speaking, I wasn't very competent.

These days the fear of failure doesn't consume me like it used to. I can get comfortable with being uncomfortable. This wee farm — The Land — it's ours. If we ruin it, we haven't ruined it for someone else; we've only ruined it for ourselves.

That childhood conversation with myself played on my mind for the rest of my life. Over the years, people have always been keen to lend me things or let me have a go with their flash new toy, and most of the time I've declined their generous offers. The thinking being, if I didn't use whatever it was I couldn't scratch it, or break it, or ruin it. As I've got older, though, I've come to realise that because of this mindset I've missed out on stuff. Another reason I wanted to go farming is so I could try my hand at a whole lot of practical tasks. These days the fear of failure doesn't consume me like it used to. I can get comfortable with being uncomfortable. This wee farm — The Land — it's ours. If we ruin it, we haven't ruined it for someone else; we've only ruined it for ourselves.

AS KIDS, THE FARMING DIDN'T finish once we were inside. The phone would ring right up until ten o'clock at night. 'Good evening, Matt Chisholm speaking. How can I help?'

'Is your old man home?'

'No, I'm sorry, he's not. Can I take a message?'

I would talk for ages on the phone to some of Dad's colleagues or clients about farming and footy. Given my insatiable appetite for farming,

Previous page My good mate Willy McSkimming in action with the shears.

my parents would loan me out to farmers around the district. I'd go and stay with the Herberts or the Davises even though they didn't have any kids my age. It didn't seem to matter where I was, as long as I was scratching the itch.

I also ran a reasonably large farming operation on the living-room floor. I must've had hundreds of small plastic farm animals. You could buy them at the stationery shop for 25 cents each. I had fences, too, made out of ice-block sticks and glue. My oldest brother, Dean, even built some pretty handy tractors and stock trucks to cart those farm animals around in. They were trucks that Dick Knight would've been proud to drive. A couple of them actually ended up as ornaments in the local Ford dealership.

FOR US KIDS, COUNTRY LIFE was good — and it wasn't all about work, either. We'd go spotlighting for eels, then take 'em round to the local shearing contractor so he could smoke 'em. We wouldn't have known about eel sushi back then. We'd catch freshwater lobsters and cook 'em up as soon as we pulled 'em out of the creek. Of course, you'd need dozens of the wee buggers for a decent feed. We also had a ball riding motorbikes and hooning around on sacks towed behind them. Well we did, right up until we got covered in cow shit. The 'game' was usually over at that point. There were only a couple of 'screens' back then, and one of them was screen printing. Good, solid, wholesome stuff. The kind of stuff some of us would want for our own kids.

When I was eleven we moved from Milton, in South Otago, to Ōamaru, in North Otago, but I still managed to keep my hand in. There was some talk about buying a wee farm, but we eventually bought another nice house with a couple of acres. I was gutted. But even as a young teenager I continued to spend an almost unbelievable amount of time out in the back paddock with my sheep. I actually increased my ewe numbers by 250%, going from six to fifteen ewes. My old, loyal huntaway Rock and

I would just mooch about, looking, smelling and listening to the stock for *hours*. I was obsessed. I was into farming more than any kid I knew, and here I was in a new area with new farms to explore, new families to stay with, different sales to go to. It seems remarkable to me now that I didn't leave school and go farming as soon as I could. As a young adult I'd run into people I knew and they couldn't believe I wasn't farming. That now seems unbelievable to me as well — why would I entertain the idea of doing anything else? But I did, and I'm not entirely sure why.

What I do know is that Dad became a little disgruntled with the rural sector in the early 1990s. I think there was a bit of a shake-up at his work that left him on the outside. Also, deregulation and the axing of farm subsidies in the 1980s was tough on rural New Zealand. The droughts that followed weren't any easier. I remember farmers killing sheep and burying them on their farms because they weren't worth anything — it cost more to transport old ewes to the freezing works than the freezing works would pay for them. Seemed like a hard way to make a living. Plus, Dad always said, 'You'll never have enough money to buy your own farm, and you wouldn't want to work for someone else, so you should think about doing something different. Become a doctor or a lawyer.' I don't think I had the smarts, or the stickability, to do either of those. Depending on the day, or who was in charge, I was either the best or the worst student in the class. I was more worried about being popular than about passing tests, plus I was pretty keen on my rugby, which sucked up a lot of time and energy. I played for and captained the Waitaki Boys' High School First Fifteen. As the smallest state boys' school in the country, we weren't a great side, but we still took it reasonably seriously.

When I was fifteen, my parents divorced and my dad and I soon stopped being best mates. I guess I lost my main link to the land. I don't think I was too worried about it at the time, though. I was busy turning into a man. I was playing footy, drinking beer and chasing girls. I partied pretty hard at school, but — after an intervention — did some work and got university entrance, and went off to Lincoln University because that's

where my mates were going and it seemed like a natural progression from Waitaki. My best mate, J, and I both planned to study for an agricultural commerce degree, but three days before we got there he found a course that didn't require any maths papers. We both signed up for a Bachelor of Social Science majoring in business and society, without knowing how that might help us in the future.

For me, university was everything you'd expect it to be for a reasonably social, rugby-playing, beer-drinking bloke from the Deep South. Although it took me an extra term, I got my degree and was immediately keen to get away from lecture theatres, books and peer pressure, so headed to the country to help my brother Dean run a wee farm and get my hands dirty again. What was supposed to be a few months of work turned into a stint of nearly two years. I could have stayed in Lawrence, West Otago forever, but I felt I should somehow use my degree and pay the government back the money I'd borrowed for my student fees, fish 'n' chips, mince and mixed veg, and booze. I'm pretty sure I was influenced by societal expectations. I'm pretty sure I felt like I had to earn the right to muck around in the country on a small bit of land.

So I had a stint working for a bank, but that was cut short when my brother Nick had a massive brainstem stroke at just 27 years of age. He wasn't able to walk or talk (and hasn't now for decades). Nick became my number one priority, and for a while there it didn't really matter what I did. With Nick's plight always in the back of my mind, I started saying 'yes' to everything. I became the 'Active Living and Event Coordinator' for the regional sports trust, Sport Otago. I even sold hair products for Wella New Zealand, because 'Beautiful hair needs an expert'. I taught English in South Korea, and travelled around the world, before coming home to study journalism in Wellington. I was excited about meeting new people and travelling to new places. Now, I felt like I had some ability and should probably start using it. I needed to prove to myself, and to others, that I was capable.

While I was studying journalism, at the age of 30, TVNZ's *20/20* show discovered Nick's story. They wanted to tell it, and they wanted me to help them. The filming, and the programme, went really well and I was asked to do some work-experience on Mark Sainsbury's *Close Up* show. That work-experience soon turned into a job. A job on national television: 7 p.m. Prime time. It was sink or swim — and after mucking about in my twenties I couldn't afford to sink. So I worked really hard until things clicked. And after things clicked I continued working really hard, because if I didn't, and just 'phoned it in', or had a bad day at the office, hundreds of thousands of people would see that I'd had a bad day at the office.

Being particularly organised and making sure everything was well planned also quashed my anxiety. It shushed the negative voices in my head that told me I didn't deserve to be there and wasn't smart enough to do this kind of work. Story-telling is a craft, and over time I got better at my craft — and every time a good story went to air I got this amazing, drug-like hit. I started collecting 'shows' like people collect items in the mall to make themselves feel better. *Close Up*, *Seven Sharp*, *Survivor NZ*, *Fair Go*, *Sunday*, *Celebrity Treasure Island*. I was finally proving to myself that I was capable — but it wasn't sustainable. I couldn't keep working the way I was working. The problem was that, for me, television was like a drug, and drugs are hard to give up. In some ways, I think I was happy being unhappy. But by the end, I was burnt out and depressed.

Story-telling is a craft, and over time I got better at my craft — and every time a good story went to air I got this amazing, drug-like hit.

After eleven years at TVNZ — eleven years of living on adrenaline and anxiety — I blew up one day. When I, rightly or wrongly, thought that I was being disrespected at work, I snapped and went berserk, both barrels blazing at anyone who looked my way. When I reached home, my wife, Elle, booked me in to see the family doctor. And when I went to the doctor I posted about it on social media: 'I'm buggered. My head hurts. It's

not working as well as it was. I'm not smiling much. Laughing even less. I promised Greg, my old workmate, before he died from depression, I'd go see the doc. It's taken me months, cos of . . . life . . . But Greg me ol' mate, today, I took that first step. #itsokaynottobeokay'

Most people would simply have taken their prescription to the chemist, gobbled up their medicine, kept their internal struggles to themselves and got on with life. Me, well, I've always been a little different. I felt like I had a responsibility to come clean. I reckon I posted about that doctor's visit for a few different reasons. First, I wanted to honour my mate Greg Boyed who'd taken his life a few months earlier. Also, for more than a decade I had made a living as a journalist who asked people to be open and honest in sharing their stories with me — but I hadn't been particularly honest myself. While I looked like one of the happiest blokes on the planet when I was on the old idiot box, I had become an expert in role-playing. At the age of 42, it had become time to be honest about my thoughts. And I'm glad I did — that social media post would eventually have an impact not only on my own life but also on the lives of thousands of other people.

For me, I'd work just one more year as a full-time television journalist before finally quitting — an unhealthy addiction put to bed. By now, I was seriously wondering how much time I had left — emails from viewers seemed full of stories about people younger than me who had been struck down with some terrible affliction. Fortunately, having slogged my guts out at TVNZ for twelve years, I felt as though I had proved myself. I could finally give myself permission to go and live my dream. Fortunately, I had found someone who shared that dream. And fortunately, we had a plan. A road to travel on.

THE START OF THE ROAD

I once met a guy who said that we should look at life as if it were a two-week holiday. In the first week of the holiday — the first half of your life — most people want to go and meet as many other people as possible. Try as many restaurants and beaches as they can. In the second week of the holiday, they tend to hang out with people they click with, go to restaurants that suit their taste, visit beaches they like. When I turned 40, with my first child, Bede, finally on the ground, I felt like I was ready for the second week of my holiday. I was ready to raise some animals and children on a small piece of land.

Not long after Elle and I met, we started regularly visiting her parents, Dennis and Christine, on their farm at Tiger Hill, in the Manuherikia Valley in heartland Central Otago. For me, it was such a good antidote to Auckland and the newsroom. We'd fly to Queenstown and immediately beeline it for the much more laid-back Alexandra, Clyde, Ōmakau, Ophir and Chatto Creek. It was real; nothing flash about it. The people were the salt of the earth. It was like Milton, only much hotter in the summer and much colder in the winter. It was like Southland (where Elle grew up), only much hotter in the summer and much colder in the winter. We both thought it would be a great place to bring up kids.

I would try to help Dennis with mustering or working with the cattle in the yards. We'd swim in the river or the pool. We'd drink coffee in the cafes. We'd go exploring: the Poolburn dam; Naseby; St Bathans; the Maniototo. Compared with Auckland and the newsroom, of course, it was calm. It was peaceful. It was also one of the most beautiful places I'd ever seen, and some of it was for sale. Dennis was grazing a couple of small blocks at Chatto Creek, and one of them had been on the market recently. We drove over it with him.

'This wee block here's the best one,' he said. 'It was for sale, but he took it off the market. It's 33 acres, so that's 13 hectares. You might pick it up for less than quarter of a million.' Thirty-three acres of paradise was half the price of a small Auckland house section. We found the owner, phoned him, and bought it. It was 2015.

But 33 acres wasn't enough. I'd always wanted 50, and when it comes to living your dream you don't do things by half. Three years later, in 2018, we bought the neighbour's 54 acres, giving us 87 acres in total, and the right to build two houses. Of course, we only needed one. The plan was to carve off and sell 15 acres, which would leave us with 72 acres, or 29 hectares. Dennis would farm it for us until we'd had enough of the rat race. We bought that second block off a woman whose husband had died before they were able to go and live their lifestyle block dream. I didn't want that to happen to us. Every time we had to return to Auckland it became harder and harder to leave Central Otago, especially once we had the boys.

Bede was born in 2016; Finn in 2018. We didn't really have any family in the big smoke, but in the Manuherikia Valley Elle's parents were over the fence and just down the road. Her sister Bridget and brother-in-law Rhys and their children, Jesse and Mia, were just down the other road. My mum, Joss, was a couple of hours away by car and so was my brother Nick and his family. We were always going to leave Auckland for Chatto Creek; the big question was when.

I had been brought up to work hard, to make the most of my opportunities. I guess most of us in this country have. Our careers are

meant to come first, or at the least higher up on the list than a hobby — and our 29 hectares at Chatto Creek were never going to be anything more than just a hobby. The average size of a sheep and beef farm in New Zealand ranges from around 200 hectares for fertile, highly productive farms to over 1,500 hectares in the hill country of the South Island. In our area, an economic unit probably needs to be about 700 hectares. A lot more than our 29. But even if I'd wanted to be a full-time farmer, we could never afford to buy a real farm (despite what you might think about the kind of money TV people make).

By leaving TVNZ for the hills, I was essentially putting our lifestyle before making a living. We weren't entirely sure how we were going to pay the bills. At that stage I had a contract with TVNZ's *Sunday* programme to tell three stories a year; I was also the co-host of *Celebrity Treasure Island*, but with declining TV audiences, no one really knew how many seasons that show had left. On top of that, as a host, I was merely a contractor with few rights. If Warner Brothers decided, for whatever reason, that I was no longer the right person for the job, I'd be down the road without a say in it. I had also been asked to host a TV show on men's mental health and write a book. Neither of those projects would be big earners. And, once we were living in the sticks, would I even want to make television?

By leaving TVNZ for the hills, I was essentially putting our lifestyle before making a living. We weren't entirely sure how we were going to pay the bills.

On the other hand, what did I have to lose? I'd achieved almost everything I wanted to achieve in the media game; yet, in the end, I'd never been so unhappy. Arguably, once we left Auckland the worst thing that could happen was I'd be unhappy in a different place. I've always been a sucker for the philosophical — for those sayings you find in the *Chicken Soup for the Soul*–type books. So many of them resonate with me. One has really stuck; it's a saying I've tried to live by ever since I first read it.

And it goes: 'Life is merely a dash between two numbers. The year you're born and the year you die.' For most of us, of course, the year we die is an unknown. The saying means that you have to make the most of the dash. I've always wanted to make the most of the dash — if we only had one life, I was going to live a bloody good one. Even though I wasn't always sure what a good life looked like.

Whether I was a hairy-arsed teenager playing footy, a scarfie downing booze at the bar, a wide-eyed traveller checking out the best — and the worst — the world had to offer, or an overthinking journo in an inner-city newsroom, I've always thrown the kitchen sink at that bloody dash. Experiences have always been more important to me than money. I've always tried to say 'yes' more than I've said 'no'.

But when you live fully, when you're always having a red-hot go, it doesn't always work out. I'd often come second playing rugby, especially at school. The booze took me to some dark places; it actually got so bad that I finally hung my glass up for good. Travelling the world was fun and enlightening, but I soon learnt that wherever I went I would be there. That is, it didn't matter whether I was in the South Island or Switzerland, I still had to put up with me.

The journalism and reality TV was a phenomenal experience that took me all over the country and all over the world, satisfying my curiosity and fuelling my ego, but in the end, it wasn't the lifestyle I wanted for my family.

I always knew I'd become a farmer in the end. Of all the many things I've wanted to do with my life, farming was the one I wanted to do more than anything else. On a small scale, though. I imagine that most farmers would want to run the biggest operation they could financially and physically handle, but I've never thought like that. I've never wanted my livelihood to depend on farming. Leaving so much up to unpredictable gods and volatile overseas markets? No thanks — that shit's not for me, I'm far too risk-averse for that. I reckon those big operators with multi-million-dollar mortgages have balls of steel. They're probably what my high-school economics teacher called 'Rational Economic Man'. Me, I've never been too worried about economics. And I've never been very rational. I'm driven by emotion and a real desire to experience life: the good *and* the bad. I was once chewing the fat with a female friend in Auckland, when she said, 'What's the point in owning land that you can't make any money from?' As hard as it was not to reply sharply, I bit my tongue and just thought: *I think you've missed the point of life.* But you don't know what you don't know — you don't know what anything is really like until you have a go at it.

Starting out, my farming knowledge was pretty much limited to that of a fifteen-year-old kid from 1991, and while I could *talk* about a lot of things, I couldn't actually *do* that much.

In going on this adventure, we'd find the answers to so many questions. Starting out, my farming knowledge was pretty much limited to that of a fifteen-year-old kid from 1991, and while I could *talk* about a lot of things, I couldn't actually *do* that much. So: how hard would it be to farm 72 acres in one of the coldest *and* hottest parts of the country? Would I be practical enough to do a lot of the physical work required? Being a sensitive bugger, how well would I handle the whole 'when you've got livestock, you've got dead stock' thing? How would I pay the bills? How much time would the farm take up? Would it get in the way of me actually paying the bills? Would it put pressure on our marriage? Would the kids enjoy it? Would we get closer, or further away, from achieving a good work–life balance? How well accepted would we be in our new community? What would going farming mean for my mental health? Would I feel like I'm making a big enough contribution to the world?

Would it all be worth it in the end?

WE ENDED UP OWNING LAND for four and a half years before we could start playing on it. That gave me masses of opportunity to waste a heap of time getting excited about going country — I'd already been keeping old clothes for years because they'd 'come in handy on the farm one day'. When I turned 42, Elle gave me the best present I've ever had — a laminated A3-size Google Earth photo of our land. It wouldn't have cost any more than ten bucks, but it was a gift that kept on giving. I've spent hundreds, maybe thousands, of hours looking at that photo. I'd try to figure out where our house, sheds, yards and paddocks would go. Using whiteboard marker pens and scale rulers, I'd scribe lines on the laminate, then change my mind, rub it all out and start again. I'd crunch numbers and draw lines until I fell asleep over the photo.

This place, the place that would become known as 'The Land' simply because that's just what we always called it, was an obsession even before we got there.

The dream of a five-year-old kid, cherished for 40 years.

I couldn't wait to start breeding farm animals. So before we went country, I spent a lot of time researching different breeds of sheep, cattle, pigs and chickens. I'd google 'images' and 'breeds' well into the night until the images were blurry and I couldn't see out of my eyes.

Initially I was interested in breeds that I liked the look of, as opposed to having any commercial characteristics. Some breeds have stuck with me since before I'd even started school. Others, like Highland cattle, I fell for while travelling the world. I once filmed a TV story on viticulturist Peter Yealands, who played classical music to his vines because he reckoned it helped them grow better grapes and produce better wine. As weird as I found that, I was more interested in the cute little Babydoll Southdown sheep he had grazing underneath those vines.

After some late-night googling, I came across a Babydoll breeder in South Auckland who offered me a 'start-up breeding package' — I think it was about seven sheep — for a whopping $80,000. When I read the email, I almost spat out my over-priced coffee all over my computer. As obsessed

and passionate as I am, I was never going to pay *that* kind of money for animals that could die in their sleep.

I discovered Swiss Valais Blacknose, beautiful sheep with fluffy white wool, black points and curly horns, at the Auckland A&P Show. Purebreds were fetching similar money to the Babydolls — ten grand for females. Ridiculous. I also discovered Speckle Park cattle, an attractive-looking cattle beast out of Canada, relatively new to New Zealand. Black with white-speckled coats or white with black points, they were the Valais of the cattle world. I was hooked. I didn't have to look far to find some, either: Dennis had some Speckle Parks just over the fence from our place. But he sure didn't make buying them easy.

SHIFT TO ŌMAKAU

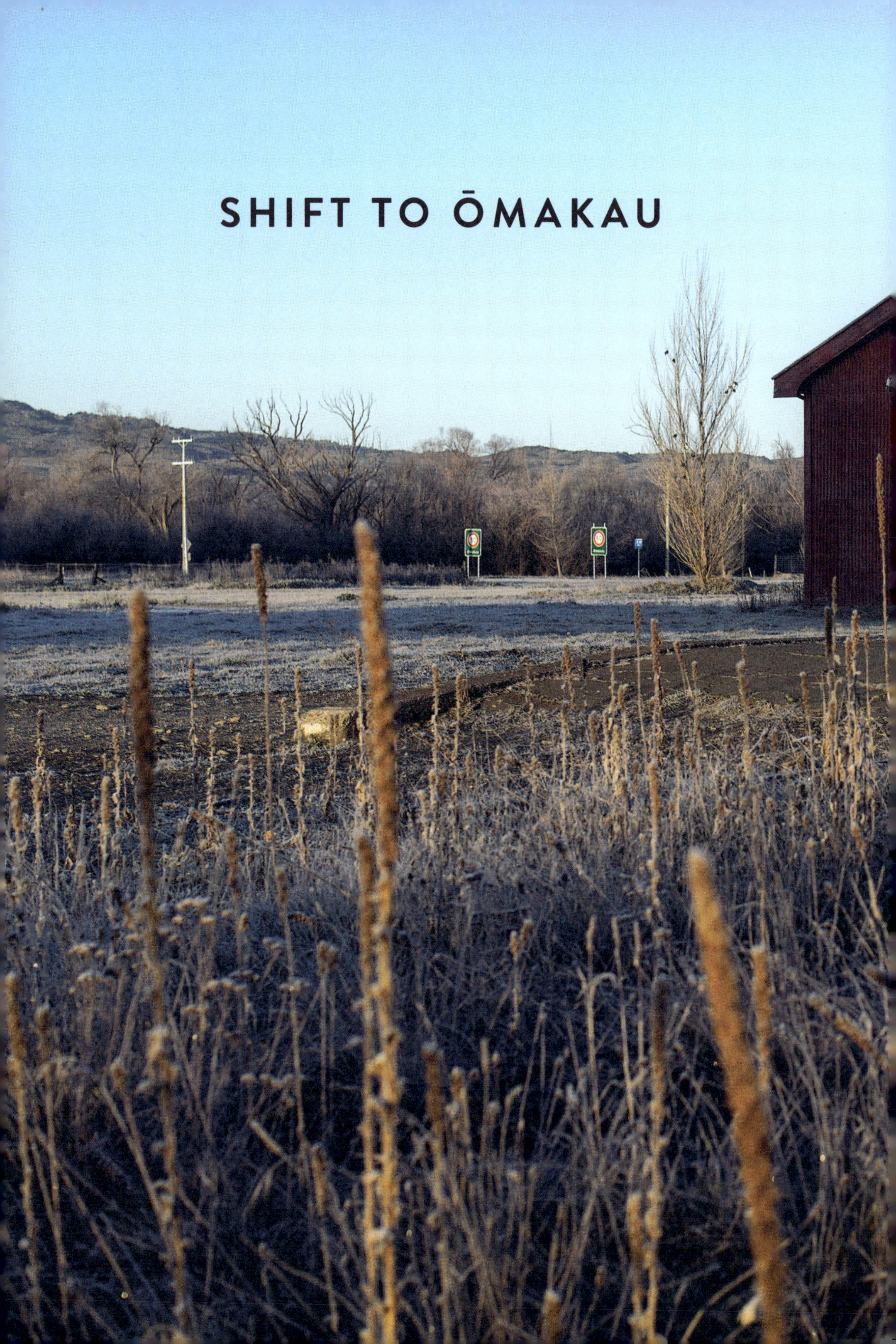

OMAKAU

THE LAND

After those few years of feeling 'stuck' in Auckland and in the newsroom, and of worrying about whether or not it would all work out, we finally took the plunge and headed for the hills at the end of 2019. We spent the first two and a half years living in a small rental property in Ōmakau, about a five-minute drive from our farm at Chatto Creek. It became a road well travelled.

When we arrived south, at what was rather short notice, Dennis had 85 of our then 87 acres in crop for grazing his cattle through the winter. This left us the ugliest 2 acres in Central Otago to play with — a terrible-looking wee triangle paddock full of culverts, humps and hollows, too wet in some places and too dry in others, right on State Highway 85 between Ōmakau and Alexandra.

It might sound ridiculous, but that ugly wee paddock was all I wanted starting out, and it was enough to really blow my hair back. It needed a bit more fencing and some stock water before it was good to go. We had to rope in 'Robbo', our neighbour-cum-digger-driver and sometimes entertainment, who is also my relative because his mum and my dad are first cousins. (We're not all interbred here, just some of us.) Robbo, who has been driving diggers since he could walk, is kind of hyperactive. He's got ants in his pants. One day he dug a nice big hole in the triangle paddock, and then he and I hooked up hundreds of metres of pipe and ran water from his place to fill it so that in the future, the animals in the paddock would have something to drink. Drinks in hand, we both sat patiently by that hole for a while, waiting for the water to come. Having done the work and with the sun going down, we wanted to make a real moment of it — two cousins, two cobbers, living the dream — but the water never came. There were six or seven lengths of pipe and we hadn't connected up every one of them. So we had to put down our drinks and fix things.

With the hole eventually full of water, Robbo put his cattle in the paddock to chew out the long, rank grass and allow some new grass to start growing, but it took its sweet time. By this stage I'd become quite close with Alan Parker, known as 'AP', who worked for Dennis and Christine on their farm at Tiger Hill. We'd often catch up at smoko time or over the fence. AP owns a wee bit of dirt down the road at Millers Flat, and being a bit longer in the tooth than me he'd seen a thing or two in his time. He had spent a few years in the Australian mines, where I'm pretty sure he worked — and played — reasonably hard. (Old cobbers of his, reading that last line, would probably laugh until their tears rendered the words on the page unreadable, thinking, *That's one hell of an understatement.*) AP is a real playful character who loves a drink, a smoke, a laugh and, sometimes, a good deep chat. With our similar personalities, and a shared love of the land, we clicked immediately.

AP could see how important that little 2-acre paddock was to me and wanted to help me crank it up. One day when he was drilling in new grass seed for Dennis, he swung by and did a few laps in my triangle paddock, direct-drilling the seed over the old grass. It seemed like a great idea, but initially it didn't look like it: the old thatchy grass probably hadn't been touched in a hundred years and the drills ripped a lot of it out of the dirt. By the time AP had buttoned off the tractor, I had a bare paddock with some huge clumps of what had once been grass. It looked like my worst enemy had released dozens of angry wild pigs on to the property. I was gutted. It was hard to believe, but the ugliest paddock in Central Otago — right on this busy piece of road for everyone to see — had become even uglier. I was devastated. There were tears in my eyes as I raked those clumps of old grass up into piles.

AP's experience told him everything would turn out okay. My inexperience told me it wouldn't. Now AP wanted to throw what I thought was good money after bad (even though none of this had cost me anything), and follow up the seed with some lime. But when he went to throw the lime around with the spreader, it had got wet because of some uncharacteristic recent rain and wouldn't go through the machine. It didn't matter to AP. 'We'll just throw it out by hand,' he said. So we did. One weekend, bucket after bucket, he and I threw lime on that wee 2-acre triangle paddock. Bucket after bucket. And as we worked, bucket into the lime, hand into the bucket, lime on to the paddock, AP and I talked and laughed the whole day. And unbelievably — at least to me — that wee paddock eventually came right. When the first wee lines of almost fluorescent green grass came sprouting through the terra firma, I couldn't have been happier. I once asked AP why he wanted to give up his weekend — an opportunity to get away from the farm — to do more 'farming', and he answered, 'I just want to hang out with you. I just want to talk to you. I just want to laugh with you.' There really are some good people in this world. AP no longer works for Dennis and Christine; he's moved back home to the Teviot Valley. I miss him.

FOR THE NEXT COUPLE OF years, I collected sheep and cattle with reckless abandon. By this stage I had gone off the Babydoll Southdowns and was sold on the new-style Southdowns. When I was a kid helping Dad in the yards in Milton, I remember seeing a Southdown lamb and loving the look of it. It was a chunky, well-muscled wee bugger with a bit of wool on its face, and a mousey-brown nose and legs. One of my new farm advisers, Google, told me that the Southdown, a meat sheep, was a

very old and pure breed out of England, which had helped in developing a number of other breeds. 'It has been of particular importance in New Zealand, where it was used in the breeding of the Canterbury lamb. In the twenty-first century it is kept principally as a terminal sire', meaning that Southdown rams were used over other breeds of sheep to produce meaty lambs. Appreciating the back story, I asked around. Everyone kept saying the same thing: 'Yeah, everyone used to have Southdowns, but most people went out of them because they were too small and fat. But now they've stretched them out and they're making a real come-back.'

I remembered that a mate from university, Fraser Fletcher, used to breed them. Fraser lives just down the road from AP, in Heriot, so I reached out to him; but twenty-odd years on, he wasn't involved with them any longer. 'Though,' he said, 'Blair Robertson, with the Merrydowns stud, is the biggest Southdown breeder in the world and he's just down the road near Tapanui.' Everyone around here lives just down the road from someone else. Another call to an old footy cobber, Don Murray — who happened to be the president of the Southdown Sheep Society — confirmed that Blair would see me right. Don planted a reasonably fertile seed that day: 'You should start a Southdown stud, Chis. You only need ten ewes and you can start a stud. It looks pretty cool having the name of your farm on their ear tags.'

I rang Blair. 'It's Matt Chisholm here from Chatto Creek.'

He must've thought he was being pranked. 'What, the fella off the telly?'

'Yeah, that's right. I want to buy half a dozen stud Southdown ewes off you . . . Will you sell them to me?'

Long story short, he did. Months later, in May 2020, Blair arrived with six in-lamb Southdown ewes, which had been running with his best Southdown ram. They were fine-looking Southdown sheep carrying soon-to-be-born purebred Southdown lambs. When they leapt off the back of his ute, it felt like some kind of mid-winter Christmas party.

Not long afterwards, I received a call from North Canterbury. When we'd left Auckland for Central Otago, I'd taken a detour to look at some sheep, having learnt of a way to get into Swiss Valais Blacknose without paying ten grand for a single animal. I could do it by 'breeding up'. The North Canterbury guys were selling first cross, or 50% Valais, ewe hoggets (these are one-year-old sheep) that had been mated to a purebred ram. A few days after they appeared on *Country Calendar*, I received the call. 'G'day, Matt, Hayden Cowan here. Do you still want a couple of in-lamb ewes?'

Even though I had just eight sheep on that terrible little triangle paddock on State Highway 85, I couldn't have been any more excited about my first lambing in 30 years.

Weeks later, two 50% Swiss Valais Blacknose ewe hoggets, both in lamb with twins, arrived. I paid $1,380 (including GST) each for them, plus a bit of cartage to get 'em to Central from Canterbury. Not much change out of three grand for just two sheep. However, the idea was that in the first lambing I'd get four lambs that were 75% Valais, and chances are that two of them would be girls. The following year I'd mate those two girls with a purebred ram and end up with lambs that were 88% Valais. And so on. After just five years of 'breeding up', of which the first one had been done for me, I ought to have sheep that were 97% Swiss Valais Blacknose, which I could call purebred.

Even though I had just eight sheep on that terrible little triangle paddock on State Highway 85, I couldn't have been any more excited about my first lambing in 30 years. However, my first lamb on the place was neither a Southdown nor a Valais. After filming my first *Country Calendar* story I brought home a mis-mothered Polwarth lamb from Loch Linnhe Station near Kingston. 'Polly the Polwarth', who was initially super-friendly but isn't that friendly anymore, has produced six cracking lambs in three seasons.

In that first year on the farm, I wintered my Southdown and Valais-cross ewes on 100-year-old thatchy grass and overpriced lucerne hay until they started popping out lambs. The Southdowns were first, and there were plenty of them. Two here, three there . . . and bloody good lambs they were, too. Each one received a nice wee woollen jacket, was tagged, and got written up in the diary. But there was a problem. What was I meant to do if a ewe had three lambs, given that she only had two teats? I took a poll. Turns out a lot of breeders take one of the three lambs home and bottle-feed it. Within a few days I bloody nearly had more lambs at home than I did in the paddock, and initially I was feeding those lambs five times a day.

Even though it's really a kid's job, there's something quite nice about bottle-feeding lambs. It's a great way to practise mindfulness — but when you're doing it five times a day, it feels like you're just finishing off feeding your lambs and moments later you have to start all over again. It feels like you don't have any time to get anything else done. Anyway, the first five Southdown ewes produced eleven live lambs, and even though I was doing all that bottle-feeding, I was pretty bloody happy with a lambing percentage, albeit a premature one, of 220%. (Farmers work out lambing percentages by dividing the number of lambs at tailing time by the number of ewes that went to the ram.)

But there was one ewe left to lamb, 514/15 — the hungriest, pokiest, most arrogant ewe on the place. With a small udder and birthing juice hanging out of her oversized bits for days, I eventually figured out she'd need help getting her big single lamb out. But I needed help, too, so I rang Dennis. When you're in the shit it's hard to beat Dennis, because he is a smart, practical man, and at 70 he's been there, done that. Anyway, Dennis chipped away, with his silver-haired 70-year-old carcass lying on that thatchy old grass, his big hard-working hands up 514/15, red in the face, grunting and groaning for what seemed like about an hour, until he finally pulled out what must have been an 8- or 9-kilogram lamb — as dead as the Labour Party was in the 2023 election. And at that moment Dennis looked up at me, panting with the effort, and said: 'There's a bloody reason

150ML
200ML
250ML
300ML
350ML
400ML
500ML
550ML

why . . . *huh huh huh* . . . everyone got out of these bloody Southdowns, Matt.' And as he walked away through the livestock, he turned and said: 'And take those silly coats off the bloody lambs — they look bloody ridiculous.'

Those lambs, though — eleven from just six ewes, giving me 183% — grew like Mike Tyson's children, with muscles on their muscles, and were put together as well as Princess Kate Middleton. Just two months later, I got a text from Christine. 'Dennis wants to know if you're putting your Southdown lambs in the show?'

Smiling from ear to ear, I replied, 'Didn't think Dennis liked Southdowns.'

'Well,' she came back, 'he likes the look of your ones.'

I was out of the ute and in the paddock chasing around the new-born lambs like a kid in a candy store . . . and was gutted when the first new lamb I saw was a ram.

Because of my TV commitments, it would be a couple of years before I'd enter any Southdown sheep in any shows, but when I eventually did, it would have to be one of the most satisfying things I've ever done.

The Southdown lambing was over by early September, and the two much younger Valais wouldn't lamb until a few weeks later. It was a long wait, mainly because the sex of those lambs was a whole lot more crucial. If the ewes produced ewe lambs, I'd be a year closer to breeding full-blooded Valais sheep; if not, then not. One day the first hogget lambed, and its first lamb was a ram — and so was the second. I was a little disappointed, but happy that both were alive and kicking. I was away making telly when the second Valais ewe lambed. As soon as I was home, I rushed down the road to check 'em out. I was out of the ute and in the paddock chasing around the new-born lambs like a kid in a candy store . . . and was gutted when the first new lamb I saw was a ram. Surely

I wouldn't have four out of four ram lambs? I sighted the second new lamb and thought I could see a wee ball bag hanging between the hind legs. I caught him, flipped him over, and confirmed my fear. My two Valais ewes had produced four ram lambs. I was still at least five years away from producing full-blooded Valais sheep. Nature, eh? I had to laugh.

Regardless, my first lambing in a long time was a good one. Those eight sheep produced fifteen lambs, a respectable 188%. The biggest shame, I suppose, was that I didn't have 8,000 ewes rather than eight.

IT HADN'T TAKEN LONG FOR The Land and the livestock to become like a drug, with me always after my next hit. Compared with Auckland and the newsroom, I seemed to have a bit more time. I was always finding reasons to make the five-minute journey south from Ōmakau to the farm; I'm pretty sure I started looking for any excuse I could to leave home and head down to that 2 acres. Initially, through winter, I had to feed the sheep some hay and keep moving the electric fence to give them a fresh pick of grass. Then in spring I had to do a lambing beat, of course — I had to make sure that the ewes weren't having trouble birthing and the new-born lambs were getting a drink from their mums. Once we'd finished lambing I started 'irrigating' that wee paddock, by simply taking the hose that led to the stock water pond and placing it in different spots on the land. I picked up rocks. I cut down thistles.

When the boys came with me, they'd throw rocks into the pond or make 'birthday cakes' out of cow shit. I'll write it again: they made 'birthday cakes' out of cow shit. It's a shame we lose our imagination, isn't it? I would try to take the boys as often as I could, but they didn't always want to go. Central Otago can be bitterly cold in winter and sometimes there's no place like home with Mum. When they did come, though, 90% of the time they loved it. They'd help me feed the lambs and calves. 'I want to hold the bottle, Dad . . . *Dad* — Bede held the bottle last time.' They'd help me chase the animals. They soon started making the same sounds

their dad made to move the livestock on. 'Hey hey hey hey . . . Phit phit phit phit . . . Come on come on come on.' With their windows down they'd slap the side of the ute, *bang bang bang*. Occasionally, just occasionally, they'd use some of Dad's naughty farm words: 'Come on, you fucking evil little bastard.'

The more they were able to help, the more they enjoyed it. When I was 'drafting' — separating some of the sheep off from others in the yards — their job was to keep the sheep up to me. It's not easy for kids who weigh 18–22 kg to move animals four times their size in the right direction, but they'd do it. 'This is great fun. This is the best day ever!' they'd say. They've now had at least a hundred best days ever. And the best days ever just keep coming. When I'm taking down or putting up electric fences, they want to help me put the standards in or help me take the standards out of the ground. They help me pace out the 7 or 8 metres between each standard. They're always asking, 'I'm helping eh, Dad?' Or, 'Am I doing a good job, Dad?' Well, the boys might have been born in Auckland, but it didn't take long for them to turn into country kids.

All told, I was spending an unbelievable amount of time in that triangle paddock on State Highway 85 between Ōmakau and Alexandra, and everyone seemed to know it was ours. Even if I was only there for half an hour, I reckon half a dozen people would drive past tooting and waving. Some would stop for a chat; I enjoyed that. Meanwhile, I was always looking over the fence at the rest of our farm, the other 85 acres that Dennis was grazing, wondering when he'd hand it over.

BRINGING HOME THE BACON

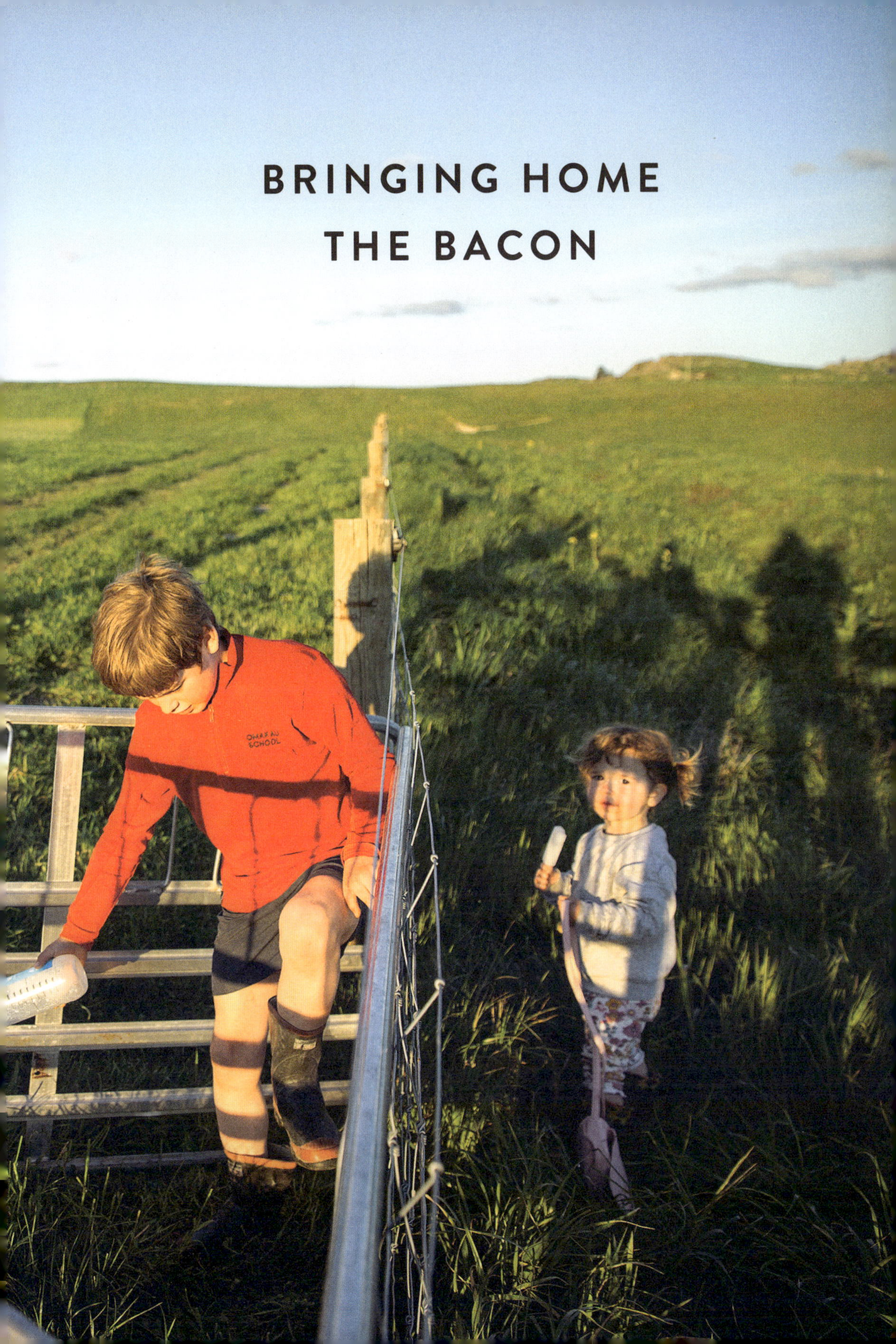

As much as we'd wanted to move to heartland Central Otago, it was bloody hard for me to leave Auckland and my television career behind. Making telly is like a drug, and drugs are hard to give up. It can be so incredibly rewarding — sometimes it felt like we were able to make a real difference with our stories.

Everyone at dinner parties wanted to talk television, but in the end I didn't have the desire or the energy to go to the dinner parties. That said, though, if I wasn't 'Matt from the telly' then who was I? But given that Matt from the telly was unhappy, Matt and his family had nothing to lose by going. It took a lot of overthinking and toing and froing before we eventually gave it a crack, even though I still wasn't entirely sure how we'd pay the bills.

At this point I was a co-host on *Celebrity Treasure Island*, had a contract with *Sunday* to do three stories a year (rather than the full-time role I had been doing), was going to host a Movember-funded two-part documentary series on men's mental health and depression, and was going to write a book about my life. But my family and our life on 'The Land' was now my priority. Our wee 'farm' is a bloody good way of spending money but not such a good way of making it, so that wasn't the answer to how we were going to pay the bills. Throughout my life, when it came to making a living you could well say that I haven't been that proactive, that I've just taken up opportunities that have come my way.

And, luckily, there were more of these to come. Towards the end of 2020 and our first year out of Auckland, a bloke my dad had worked with 35 years ago jumped into my direct messages. This bloke, Mike Green, wanted me to emcee a big Rural Support Trust fund-raiser in New Plymouth. Think 300-odd people, black tie, white shirts, red dresses, perfect hair and make-up, fine food and sparkling wine. Mike headed up the RST in Taranaki. It's a charitable organisation of rural people helping other rural people through tough times. If country folk were struggling with an adverse weather event, their health or wellbeing, financial pressures, employment issues, or animal welfare problems, someone from the RST would be there to help.

I could say many things about Mike Green, but the first one that comes to mind is that he's bloody determined. He had been following my career pretty closely. He'd got wind of the documentary and book coming out and wondered if I'd be prepared to tell 'my story' as well as emcee the event. The trust would fly Elle and me to New Plymouth, put us up for a couple of nights, and fly us home with a little bit of spending money to boot. 'Look, Matt, farmers are going through a pretty tough time at the moment, and I reckon if you told your story you could really help a lot of people.'

I wasn't sure about this. While I was prepared to talk about my struggles with the bottle and the black dog in a book and on the telly, I reckoned it would be much harder to do in front of a live audience. Plus I'd have to write some sort of speech at a time when I was already under the pump writing that book. But I kept thinking about that 'helping a lot of people' line and how I have a responsibility to make a decent contribution while I'm alive. I kept thinking about how I should turn my negative experiences into positive ones if and where I can.

EVENTUALLY, GREENY'S PERSISTENCE paid off. One Friday in November 2020, Elle and I farmed out the kids and flew to New Plymouth. I was still working on my speech. 'Hey,' I said to Elle, 'you know how I told you how I thought I might've been HIV-positive once back when I was drinking?'

'Yes,' she replied, sounding worried.

'Well, I slept with a prostitute in Vietnam but didn't realise I'd slept with a prostitute until she demanded money in the morning.'

Surprised, she asked: 'And you're going to tell people that?'

'Yep — if I'm going to tell this story, my story, I can't sugar-coat it. It has to be warts and all. I have to listen to the advice I've given people as a journalist for the past dozen years — that's how I'm going to reach people and actually make a difference.'

Right from the start I knew I'd offend a few people with my honesty, but I also knew that that honesty would resonate with the majority. I knew it would actually help bring people along with me and help make a difference.

I finished writing that speech with just minutes to spare, which is pretty typical for me. By now I'd been telling stories on TV for twelve years, and had a good handle on what worked. I always want to make people laugh, but tonight I also wanted to make them feel. I wanted to make them think about their own lives, or the lives of the people they love, and think about how they might be tracking.

As I walk to the lectern with my freshly printed script — my life story in sixteen pages — Taranaki's who's who is staring up at me. The good thing about making telly is that the audience isn't there while you're filming. Now, I can almost taste the imposter syndrome in my mouth but there's no turning back. My first job is to welcome the crowd — in my own way — and quickly make them laugh; quickly get them on my side. So: a short gag about me being hopeless down on the farm. The audience responds immediately. They're picking up what I'm putting down. They're on my side; they want me to succeed. And they're laughing. I'm in charge

of the delivery. I can speed up, or slow down, for effect. It's on.

I heard that audience laugh and I watched them cry. And I cried with them. Over and over again. And when they were crying, I snapped them out of it with a laugh. It was fun and it was raw and it was emotional, and when I finished about 45 minutes later those 300-odd people stood up from their chairs and clapped their hands in front of their smiling, teary faces. Like almost everything I do in life, I had given it everything I had. Rightly or wrongly, I left no stone unturned and I was exhausted. I was so buggered, actually, that I could barely eat my dinner.

Like almost everything I do in life, I had given it everything I had. Rightly or wrongly, I left no stone unturned and I was exhausted.

Mike Green took over the remaining emcee duties, and after the meal I was inundated. Dozens of people patiently queued up to talk to me. They thanked me. And they hugged me. And they told me that my story was their story. I actually ran out of time to talk to everyone because there was another speaker to come and there was an auction and there was a debate, but in between all of that, in the breaks, more people came and patiently queued up to talk to me. And when the night was officially over they came up again, until Elle said 'I'm going to bed' and went. I stayed for ages, listening to everyone's story, trying to help where I could — and I started thinking: maybe *this* is what I'm here for; maybe *this* is what I'm meant to do with my life. Then, finally, I went to bed. And then I thought some more. And finally, finally, I fell asleep.

Mike Green was very appreciative of the role I'd played in that night's success. At some point he suggested that I needed to tell that story right around the country. I wasn't so sure. First, I wasn't sure that I wanted to keep telling 'my story', and then I wasn't sure about who was going to pay for it — I didn't want small rural communities having to put their hand in their pocket to hear me speak, but I couldn't spend too much time flying around the country for nothing. Greeny said, 'Leave it with me — I'll come up with something.' And he eventually did.

Shortly after the Taranaki event, my first book, *Imposter*, hit the shelves and the documentary *Man Enough* aired on our screens. I received messages from all over New Zealand, and from other parts of the world. Like: 'Your book was such a great read, I couldn't put it down. It really helped me. Thanks for reminding me what's important in life. Good luck for your new life on the land and enjoy that little family.' And from someone living in London: 'Hey mate, I've heard good things about your doco — any idea how I can view it here in England?' It was great, but while I always want to help where I can, I actually wasn't equipped to deal with many of the messages that came flooding my way and I'd have to refer people on to specialists.

Not long after this, people started approaching me about talking to their staff or catchment group or community. And every time I did a talk, another speaking engagement — or two — would come from it. I talked to Fulton Hogan's Central Otago staff in Alexandra, then their coastal team in the Catlins. Somehow I'd fallen into a new career in speaking. Someone from Celebrity Speakers got in touch: 'We'd love to have you on our books.' My diary started filling up and I was all over the country spinning yarns. At times, I didn't have much time for anything else.

THE CENTRAL OTAGO WINTER FEED Competition is held in Alexandra every second year, and someone asked if I'd speak at their 2021 event. I wasn't jumping-out-of-my-boots excited about sharing my deepest, darkest secrets with people in my new local community that I'd bump into for the rest of my life, but I figured that allowing myself to be vulnerable helps others do the same, and it might just help someone who really needed to hear the messaging. I did it. Off the back of that talk, an old acquaintance from Lincoln University, who works for ANZ, got in touch. 'One of my colleagues was at your talk in Alexandra — he reckoned it was brilliant, and I'm wondering if we could do something together.'

He and another colleague met up with Greeny and me for breakfast at the Fieldays in Mystery Creek. It was all starting to come together. Mike Green had come up with a talking tour idea, and the plan was for me to become the inaugural ambassador for the RST. The 'Time Out Tour' would see me doing 20 talks a year for three years around rural New Zealand. It would be sponsored by ANZ, Fonterra, BDO, Bayleys, Datamars Livestock and MPI. It felt like the right thing to do, so I signed up.

But on the day of my first-ever Time Out Tour talk, in Ōtautau, Southland, there was a little hiccup. The night before, I'd been in Auckland for Paddy Gower's TV3 panel on 'booze', and shared a really bad twenty-year-old story about me defecating in a sleeping bag after a heavy night on the grog. The TV producers had wanted a solid 'ice-breaker' to let the audience know that the panel wasn't just a load of pointy-headed experts, and I gave them what they wanted. The following morning, while I was sitting in Auckland Airport waiting for my flight, the call came in from Mike Green.

'Hey, did you say you shat in a sleeping bag on telly last night?'

'Something like that, Greeny, yeah,' I replied. 'Why's that?'

'We've had a call from a woman from the Southland RST, and we've also had one of the tour sponsors complain.'

'Oh yeah?' I fired back, 'Which one?'

He wouldn't tell me. 'Can you change your speech?'

My reply: 'I don't want to.'

I actually doubted that anyone from any of those organisations had complained. I stewed about it all the way from Auckland to Queenstown at 30,000 feet. Then I got off the plane and called Mike back.

'Hey, I've been having a bit of a think about this . . . and if I'm going to have Susan from Southland and Terry from Taumarunui and everyone else telling me what I can and can't say in these talks — when I'm telling *my* story — then I'm not doing these talks. I'm not doing this Time Out Tour. Simple as that.

'It's not easy telling your story, and the only way I'm going to do it is if I'm able to do it my way. Which just so happens to be the way I think we're going to reach the most people.'

I think I surprised Greeny, who quickly came around: 'What about if you put a disclaimer at the top of your speech apologising for what's going to come?' After that really anxious, stressful flight, I was more than happy with this solution.

When I eventually arrived in Ōtautau, I learnt that the Rural Support Trust representative there was a bloke called Simon Hopcroft. 'Hoppy' had been three years ahead of me at Waitaki Boys', knew my brother Nick reasonably well, and had a pretty good gauge on what I was like. I told him about the complaint and asked him what he thought I should do.

'You just tell your story, mate,' he replied, 'and tell it your way. I'm sure whatever you do, it'll be a hit here.'

Hoppy had told me what I wanted to hear and given me permission to be a bit naughty. He also gave me a name — his name — that I could use for a few of my gags, which went down well with the Western Southland audience. After the talk I was quick to hit up individuals from the major sponsors and ask them what they thought. 'It was brilliant,' one of them said. 'Perfect,' said another. In this new PC world, I could get away with being very un-PC. I could be me.

OVER THAT YEAR I FRONTED twenty Rural Support Trust Time Out Tour talks from Stewart Island to Whangārei. I even did a couple on the Chathams. I spoke to groups of 450 people in flash new auditoriums, and to groups of just 50 in dinky wee community halls. And I wasn't just doing the Time Out Tour talks; I was also doing heaps of talks for businesses, especially rural ones. I started getting asked to emcee a whole lot of functions, like hosting the Eastern Rugby Club break-up in nearby Palmerston. And another break-up in the Waikato. I was a guest speaker when Southland's Tokanui club celebrated their centenary, and when the

Ohai-Nightcaps club turned 121. I hosted the Ballance Farm Environment Awards one year and the Beef + Lamb Awards the next. I hosted the 'Meat the Need' telethon. I also started facilitating workshops for businesses.

Despite hating flying, I was flying all over the place. One day I turned around from taking a pee in the Queenstown Airport toilets to see a bloke who'd been a year ahead of me at school. Jason Buchanan; we called him 'Browser' for some reason. We'd caught up for the first time since leaving Waitaki Boys' at an RST event in the Waikato a few months earlier. Now we had both missed flights because of fog and were waiting for rescheduled ones.

Browser was flying home with his family after being at his brother Willy's funeral. 'Pretty sure I'm meant to run into you right now, Chis,' he said. 'Willy has just taken his life. It's all a bit raw at the moment, but you need to keep doing what you're doing, mate.' Willy, who'd been a Southland farmer, was a year behind me at school.

I said all the things you say to someone who's just lost a family member to suicide, and then somehow we got on to the fact that my delayed flight meant I wasn't going to be able to talk to a group of farmers in South Auckland to try to stop that very thing happening. 'No way, mate,' said Browser. 'You need to talk to those people tonight. They need to hear your story and your messaging. We'll swap flights — you go on my earlier one, fly with my family, and I'll take your seat on the later flight.'

Less than a week after losing his younger brother to suicide, it would have been easy for Browser to think purely of himself and his family. But instead, he was already thinking about how he could help others. I'm forever blown away by the wonderful people in this world and their amazing acts of kindness.

So whenever I'm asked to do something — anything — nine times out of ten I say yes. Actually I'll only say no if I'm already booked.

On another level, honestly, I can't afford to say no. There's a lot of money needing to be sunk into 'The Land'.

STRETCHING OUT

The two lifestyle blocks we bought to make up our 87 acres were side by side. The dream was always to live on 50 acres — buying the second, 54-acre block in 2018 was a good decision when it came to ticking that box, but probably — at least initially — a bad decision financially. Like I said earlier, the plan was to carve off about 15 acres on the second block, with the ability to build on it, and sell it. Hopefully we'd get almost as much money for that 15-acre block as we'd paid for the entire 54. In preparing to sell that 15 acres, Dennis planted it out in new grass that needed to be grazed. I needed more stock — though, more importantly, I *wanted* more.

The reason was that I figured I'd have a much better chance of ending up with female Valais lambs if I put more ewes to the ram. Problem was, until we'd sold off that 15 acres we didn't have much money lying around so I wasn't in a position to pay the $5,000 being asked for purebred Valais rams. That didn't necessarily matter, because I'd just had four three-quarter ram lambs hit the ground. Sadly, the best-looking one decided to die one day. I don't know why. They tell me it's always either the worst animals or the best ones that die.

To carry out my plan, I needed to buy some 'foundation' ewes. These would eventually go to a purebred Valais ram when I could afford to buy one, or I could eventually put one of my new three-quarter Valais ram lambs over them, even though it wasn't within the rules of the new breed society (which didn't bother me because I'm not part of it). Dennis had some good black-faced lambs running around, some kind of Suffolk–Texel composite, and we agreed that I'd buy twenty of them. By about this stage, even I was a little worried about what was happening down on the farm. I didn't even have 50 sheep, but I had four different breeds: Southdown, Swiss Valais Blacknose, Suffolk–Texel cross and Polly the Polwarth.

I liked the idea of buying calves. First, they were cheap. Second, once you had them you could watch them develop and grow.

With my motley flock of sheep sorted for now, and always looking for something more to do down on the farm, I started thinking about cattle. I liked the idea of buying calves. First, they were cheap. Second, once you had them you could watch them develop and grow. I enjoyed bottle-feeding a few lambs, so thought I'd enjoy feeding a few calves in the triangle paddock. The thing to keep in mind here is that this was the year 2020 — the year that was almost entirely ruined by the Covid-19 pandemic. I had more time up my sleeve than I'd had for years, and I wanted to use it doing things that made me feel good. And, most of the time, farming made me feel really good.

I tried to get my hands on some new-born Speckle Park-cross heifer calves from dairy farms, but I nearly failed because I didn't get on to it until really late in the season. I wanted females because they give you more options; I'm pretty sure the only thing you can do with steers is grow them and kill them. Females can bear babies and I don't think you've really lived until you've been involved in delivering a calf. I found a dairy farmer in West Otago who was prepared to sell a couple of older Speckle Park heifer calves. I didn't really want any other breeds, but if I was going to go to all the effort of feeding calves, I reckoned it made more sense to feed five rather than two. So, I also bought two Hereford-cross heifer calves and a Speckle Park steer off him. Those five calves needed to be fed milk twice a day, and I was the one to do it. Another excuse to head down the road to 'The Land'.

Not long after I got the hang of feeding calves, Dennis gave us another one: 'Wild Bill', a wee pure-black Speckle Park bull calf that soon became a steer. He'd been mis-mothered and needed a new home. Another litre or two of milk went in the bucket. I enjoyed feeding those six calves twice a day for a couple of months, but if I'd been paying myself an hourly rate it would've been well below minimum wage. That didn't matter. With 44 sheep and six calves on 17 acres, I was still understocked and I wanted more cattle. Looking on Trade Me one night, I saw a small White Galloway heifer calf, white with black points like a white Speckle Park, for sale in Dunedin. As soon as I could get through to Dunners I would be bringing her home in the back of the ute.

I also asked Dennis about buying some of his Speckle Park heifers off him, but he wasn't that keen. 'I've got a plan for those Speckle Park heifer calves, Matt, and it doesn't involve you.'

Fortunately, I had better luck getting rid of my ram lambs than I did buying my father-in-law's calves. While it was annoying not to get any Valais ewe lambs, lifestylers loved the 75% Valais rams. The new breed society wanted members to make wethers out of impure rams, but I could do whatever I wanted. I kept one ram to put over some ewes I'd bought off Dennis and sold the other two for $500 each, which was just as well considering that their mums cost me as much as you'd pay for a cow. Normal lambs were probably being killed for about $150 to $200, so this was bloody good money.

While I was always going to keep all of my Southdown ewe lambs for breeding, I wasn't entirely sure what I'd do with my rams. I can't even remember how, now, but a true-blue local farmer, Daniel Thurlow, got wind of what we were up to on 'The Land', and came and looked at what

Top: Dan Thurlow collecting my ram lambs. **Above**: Elle and the boys feeding our calves. *Photos from Matt's personal collection*

were basically ram lambs from Merrydowns but with my tags in their ears. I kept the best one, and Dan took the other three home for $500 each. It was a seriously proud moment for me. The sheep, at least at this stage, were really paying their way.

I wanted more Merrydowns money-makers, but Blair wouldn't sell 'em. Someone put me on to his cousin, Dave Robertson, just outside of Ōamaru, and he sold me five stud Southdown ewes. With eleven, I could now start a stud — and 'The Land' Southdown stud, flock number 4538, was born. I must admit to quite enjoying seeing it all written up when the little black 'flock book' came in the mail.

IT WASN'T LONG BEFORE I found out what Dennis's plans for me were. One day he hit me up about what I was wanting to do with 'The Land' for our second winter down south. As we hadn't yet sold the block we'd subdivided off, and I was short on both cash and knowledge, I told him 'not much'. It didn't matter either way, because he had already cooked up what I felt was a relatively complicated plan.

The 2-acre triangle paddock and the 15 acres we were trying to sell weren't part of the plan. But Dennis reckoned we should plant and grow oats on the remaining 70 acres, cut it and turn it into baleage. We would pay for half of the oats to be baled, he would pay for the other half. Then we'd plant kale and under-sow it with grass, as cattle feed for the winter. He wanted us to provide the land, while he would pay for the seed and agricultural work and carry the risk. We would have half the land to graze during the winter, he would have the other half. For us it meant we would need to either buy a whole lot of cattle to graze this future crop on our half of the 70 acres, or find someone who wanted to graze it for a fee. As buying the cattle would cost about $50,000, which we didn't have, we needed to find someone who was keen to graze the crop.

So, after the oats were baled and the feed crop had grown, we were ready for someone to graze the land. But we couldn't find anyone who was keen. The crop hadn't grown as well as we'd wanted it to; we had a problem.

Fortunately, Dennis had another plan up his sleeve; not surprising, as he's always cooking up plans. This new plan, however, required *me* to graze about 70 calves on our half of our land, through the winter and into spring and summer. Dennis had calves that he needed sold. A local stock agent would buy them on behalf of a meat company at the local Ōmakau calf sale if I was prepared to graze them for the company. In winter, I'd break-feed the calves on the kale, behind an electric fence, and also give them the big bales of oaten baleage. I'd be paid on a weight gain basis.

So, after the oats were baled and the feed crop had grown, we were ready for someone to graze the land. But we couldn't find anyone who was keen.

There were several problems with this plan, though. The first was that those calves would need to be shifted every day, and I was often away from home for days. Another was that I had only recently left a newsroom and a 600-square-metre section in Auckland, had the farming brain of a fifteen-year-old and didn't really know what I was doing. On top of that, my 36-acre block didn't have a water trough. The electric fences were only 'hot' (live) if Dennis's fences on our boundary were hot, because they ran off his system. I didn't have a tractor to feed out the big bales. And where would my sheep go?

This cunning plan was pitched at the last minute, the day before the local calf sale. Dennis, of course, had a solution for every one of my problems, but the biggest problem I had was that Dennis makes a lot of sense when he talks and he's a particularly hard man to say 'no' to. Whatever I thought of his plan, I couldn't say no. But it's said you regret the things you don't do, as opposed to the things you do do — right?

I could graze 70 calves through the winter on all that crop, though I told Dennis and 'Waka', the stock agent, that I'd only be able to graze 50 calves for the meat company. If I was going to be shifting cattle every

day, I wanted at least a few of them to be mine. More than the seven I already had. And, in fact, I *could* buy a few more. At the start of 2021, I'd gone away to host *Celebrity Treasure Island*, and came home to 'The Land' in March with a pocketful of money. Just in time for the local Ōmakau calf sale.

Interestingly, the Speckle Park heifer calves that I'd wanted to buy from Dennis were at that sale. When we got there, I said to Dennis, 'You know those Speckle Park heifer calves — the ones you had a plan for that maybe didn't work out — what do you reckon they'll go for?' And Dennis replied, 'I don't know, Matt, depends on who turns up to the sale, but probably somewhere around the 700, 750, 800 dollar mark.' Then Dennis's brother Terry, a Southland stock agent who was helping sell the calves, took me away to show me Dennis's Speckle Park heifer calves. There were ten of them, second-line animals. 'Not necessarily inferior, Matt; just younger, you know,' said Terry.

Everyone's saying the right things and I start doing some maths. *Ten at 800 bucks . . . bit of GST makes it 9,200. I'd get some change out of ten grand — this'll do me*, I think.

At the start of the sale, calves are trotting in and out of the selling arena like German trains, fetching huge money. There's a real sting in the market; looks like I'll have to pay through the nose for any of Dennis's Speckle Park heifer calves. But then, for whatever reason, the sale starts slowing down. Finally it gets to 'pen 30' — Dennis's ten second-line Speckle Parks. The stock agent starts off with 'Who's got round about that 800 and go, 750 . . . 700 surely. Good-looking Speckle Park calves, the new rage, they'll move well.' Only they don't. I'm bloody sure it's because the farmers don't know what they are. They might as well have been bloody alpacas. When I tell this story, I often say they didn't know because most of the local farmers hadn't been out of the Manuherikia and Ida valleys for 50 years — which is, of course, completely untrue.

Whatever the reason, back at the sale I'm doing fist pumps on the inside. The auctioneer barks away: '550 . . . 500 . . . 450 . . . 4.' Then, someone nods to the spotter: $400 per calf. I look at Dennis, he looks at me. It's game on. 'We'll take a little 20,' says the auctioneer. I raise my hand and bid at 420. 'Who's got 440?' No one. 'Going once, going twice, sold — to the journalist.'

I bought ten Speckle Park heifer calves for $420 each. A complete steal. Apart from the fact we could've left them back at the farm, cut out the agents and the transport company, and just opened the gates between the two properties and let the calves run.

Dennis didn't hang around the sale for much longer after that, but I did — and I bought more cattle. Later that night I got on the blower to Dennis, who'd sold hundreds of calves at the sale. 'How are you going?' I asked.

'Well, I got a real hiding today — but I'm glad you got a good deal as opposed to some other bugger,' he said. Now while I can't see Dennis, I'm picking that he then leans in: 'You didn't buy those hairy bastards too, did ya?'

And I reply, 'Yeah I did, Dennis . . .'

I bought fifteen calves that day, not just Dennis's ten. At the very end of the sale, five Highland heifer calves entered the ring. Everyone looked down at them, and then immediately turned and looked straight at me and started laughing. Then came the gags. 'These will be a bit of you, Matt,' said someone. 'Perfect for you, Chis,' said someone else. They weren't wrong. I've always loved the look of Highland cattle — really fell for them when travelling around Scotland — and had been following them on Trade Me. Most farmers don't like Highland cattle because they're slow-growing. Sure, the people with lifestyle blocks like them — whether you're on 60,000 hectares or 600 square metres, most people would probably agree that Highland cattle look quite cute.

Anyway, the auctioneer cracks into it: 'Who has got around about that 500? 450 and go . . . 400?' Silence. I turn around to an old mate of mine from university, we call him 'Space', who happens to be sitting near me, and say, 'Mate, these things are going for 8 to 900 bucks on Trade Me.' And Space's old man, David, says, 'Matt, you should buy them and put 'em on

the Trade Me.' And I say to David, 'David, I've only just met you but I've already figured out you're a bloody genius' — all the while thinking, 'I don't know why *you* don't buy 'em and stick 'em on the Trade Me yourself.' Obviously he either didn't use Trade Me or couldn't be bothered mucking around with so few animals.

Regardless, down in price they go. 'Three hundred, 250, 200 . . . Bid. I'll take a little ten.' I raise my hand, and buy five Highland heifer calves for $210 each.

On the phone to Dennis that night, I say: 'But here's the rub, I bought them for $210 each, and pay for them tomorrow. I want to keep two. I've already sold the three I don't want for 850 each. I've gone from bottoming out the sale to damn near topping it.'

And of course I can't see Dennis, but I'm picking he's leaning in again: 'Shit — who sold them?'

'Matangi Station, from behind the clock in Alexandra.'

'Get on the phone, Matt, see if you can buy some more.'

I've probably told that story a hundred times, and people love that story more than any other story I tell.

NOT LONG AFTER BUYING AND selling those calves, another five Speckle Park heifer calves arrived on 'The Land'. I'd been talking to a breeder in West Otago and lined up some white Speckle Parks with black points. I paid more than twice as much per animal as I had for the ten I'd bought off Dennis at the calf sale, but I needed those calves like I needed oxygen. It meant I could have a purebred herd in just a few years. With the two bucket-fed Speckles, the ten black ones and five white ones, I was well on my way to another stud.

But when I let those five white ones out of the yards after they'd arrived on the property, they ran about 5 kilometres, doing 53 loops, and damn near jumped back on the truck they'd just walked out of. They were as mad as cut cats. On top of that, the breeder gave me different reports on how pure they were. One day they were 88% Speckle Park, the next they were just 75% — which wouldn't make a difference to most people, but made a hell of a difference to me. I decided I'd never really know for sure exactly how much Speckle Park blood they had. Either way, with all these Speckle Park heifer calves on the property I decided I'd eventually need a bull. Why would you cull females if you could breed from them and turn one beast into two? And if I was going to have a Speckle Park bull, then he'd need a paddock mate. So I'd need a Highland bull to go with the Speckle one.

Within six months I'd collected 26 calves from eight different places. I was, and still am, obsessed.

Fortunately, at this stage I was as addicted to the sheep and cattle sections of Trade Me as I was to receiving great feedback after a good TV story went to air. In no time at all I found a white Speckle Park bull calf, ostensibly fifteen-sixteenths pure, in the Nelson area. After forking out a couple of hundred dollars to pay for the three different truck trips required, he arrived. I also found a Highland bull calf near Christchurch. To pick him up, I dropped off a horse float just south of Christchurch, did a talk in Ashburton, walked out of the talk and picked up the horse float, now with the calf in it, and drove home to Chatto Creek.

If you're keeping up here, you're doing well. Within six months I'd collected 26 calves — that's 22 heifers, two steers and two bulls — from eight different places. I was, and still am, obsessed. But I figured that the Highlands, at least, were effectively free. I'd bought five at $210 each, so $1,050 in total. Sold three of those for $850 each, so $2,550 in total — meaning I was up by $1,500 before I bought the new Highland bull, 'Hamish'. After paying $890 for him, my three Highland cattle had cost me nothing *and* I still had $610 in my wallet. This is probably the only time I've made any money farming.

So, in my second year on the land I had to winter 72 calves. Hamish and 'Ice', the Speckle Park bull, were in the original triangle paddock,

eating average grass and small pieces of big round bales of oaten hay that I ripped off and threw over the fence. I had a mixed bag of nine in what I called the 'B mob', which consisted of the five original calves that I'd bucket-fed, plus Wild Bill, 'Snowy' and the two Highland heifers (which the boys named 'Ginger Nut', because one was ginger, and 'Creamy Milk', because the other was white like milk). For some unknown reason the five white Speckles ended up being wintered on Dennis's place, while I had the ten black ones that used to be his on the kale crop with the meat company's 46 steers, which also used to be his. Every morning, once the kids were sorted, I'd head down the road to 'The Land' to move the electric fences and give those calves some kale. Every couple of days, using the tractor, Dennis and Christine would feed the calves a big bale of hay.

As I've said before, it can get really cold here in winter. We're a five-minute drive from Ophir, which is supposed to be the coldest place in New Zealand. It's not the cold, though, that's the killer for me — I reckon we only get half a dozen days a year that leave you thinking *Holy hecka, this is hideous, I don't want to be doing this today* because of the weather. I'd take those days over the days when things go wrong — and when I was wintering all those cattle for the first time in my life, things often went wrong.

They weren't unforeseen things, either. The electric fence I had them behind often wasn't hot, because Dennis's big system it was running off would frequently be shorting out somewhere. Every time the fence wasn't hot the cattle would break out, and I'd have to get them back behind the wire — after figuring out where the fault was and making it hot again. This part of the farm didn't have any proper water troughs, of course; I just had an old plastic one, which the cattle beat up every day. I'd have to fence off their break *and* create a laneway for them to get to water. One time when I had to fix the water trough, after three days in a row of trying with a new part, I had to walk away for a while — I couldn't figure it out and it was driving me mad.

We did make some handy money grazing those cattle for the meat company — hundreds of dollars per animal — but it came at quite a cost. Elle and I must have been close to getting a divorce over those bloody cattle.

IN THE MIDDLE OF ALL the stuff with the cattle I had my second lambing, and if the first one was bloody brilliant at 188%, this next one didn't come close.

Our home-bred three-quarter Swiss Valais Blacknose ram, dubbed 'Roger' after Roger Federer, had done a good job over Dennis's black-face ewes. The lambs were well marked and they survived, at 135%. The offspring was 37.5% Valais. We kept the ten ewe lambs and sent their brothers to the freezing works where they fetched $175 each. I got $300 each for a few of their mothers that didn't rear lambs. Unbelievable money. As for the Southdowns, we only managed to keep thirteen lambs alive from eleven ewes — so just 118% — and we had a couple of them at home on the bottle. Without the hybrid vigour that comes with cross-breeding, they didn't perform as well. Each lamb that died broke my heart.

Those two sheep produced eight lambs in two seasons, and they were all rams. I was no further ahead in my 'breeding up' programme. It was about as funny as a fart in an elevator, but I could only laugh.

And then there were our two original Valais ewes, which produced another four lambs. And — Every. Single. One. Was. A. Ram. Again. Those two sheep produced eight lambs in two seasons, and they were all rams. Two years after buying them, I was no further ahead in my 'breeding up' programme. It was about as funny as a fart in an elevator, but I could only laugh. Again I kept the best lamb, and sold the other three for $400 each to the lifestylers. At least by this stage I had my money back after buying their expensive mothers.

Of the Southdowns, I kept five ewe lambs and my two best ram lambs. Dan Thurlow was back for another look after doing some testing on the lambs my rams had sired and he reckoned, on average, they were quite a bit heavier than lambs left by another terminal sire breed. So he bought another four of my Southdown ram lambs for $500 each. Repeat business. You beauty.

Dave Robertson then asked if I wanted to sell my best ram from the previous season at his sale in Ōamaru. It was a no-brainer, and I had a ball. I sold that ram to the Sutherlands of Benmore Station for 900 bucks. Another breeder, JJ Macaulay, who has been breeding Southdowns for 60 years, was selling a few rams at the same sale and I wanted one of them. JJ is a real character and I soon fell for him as well as his sheep; and brought one of his rams home for $2,100. Tahrua 27/20, nicknamed 'JJ', of course, was a huge ram, later described to me as an 'absolute gift'.

I'd eventually take my two best rams back to Dave Robertson's next sale, which was his last. He's now sold his Southdown stud. I sold what was easily my best ram to a new mate, Phil Smith from Glenspec Station near Naseby, for $1,000 and I sold the other one after the sale for 500 bucks. I loved those Dave Robertson sales. I enjoyed the sheep, the people, the banter, the food, catching up with my mum, and the fact that real farmers were actually buying rams off me — a journalist and public speaker — who lived on an oversized lifestyle block.

A YEAR AFTER BUYING ALL those calves at the Ōmakau calf sale, and despite not really having much money or feed, Finn and I went back to that sale. Before the auction started we discovered a wee black steer who was flying solo and on the market. Finn and I both reckoned he needed some friends, and I decided if he was going cheap, we'd bring him home.

With the real farmers not interested in fluffing around with just one animal, we picked 'Hulk' up for just 210 bucks. Mad as a snake in a sack, he pissed me off for the next nineteen months. He was really hard to shift — while all of my other cattle were quiet, Hulk couldn't be tamed. If I got within 10 metres of him he'd run 1,000 metres in the opposite direction.

It didn't take me long to figure out what to do with him in the end. One nice spring morning, when Hulk would've just turned two, Tony, the Clyde butcher, turned up and shot him dead. Considering that Hulk would've been less than 40 metres from the house when he met his maker, we really put the 'home' into home-kill that day. And, of course, that day just had to be the same day Bree had her second birthday party. At home.

So, looking out the window, ten two-year-old kids got a hell of an education on just where their food comes from. One of the reasons we'd wanted to go country was so our kids could learn this lesson. Though we probably didn't anticipate them learning it this early.

There's never a dull moment around here.

Top: Finn and 'Hulk' at the cattle auction on the day we purchased him. **Above**: Hulk's last day . . . an eye-opening lesson for the kids. *Photos from Matt's personal collection*

9

THE BEAUTIFUL GAME

I was brought up on rugby. It's been a huge part of my life. I no longer play, because I'm old and tired now, but I'm still a mad-keen spectator. Before I had the kids, I used to watch four or five games of footy every weekend. I'd watch the schoolboys, the women, the club stuff, the provincial games and, of course, the All Blacks. Actually, back in the day, if I had time I'd watch anyone: even two kids going head to head, with a pair of socks for a ball, in the hallway of their home. And while I've drifted away from professional rugby nowadays, I still love the grassroots game. Rugby is an important part of a rural community and I don't want it lost.

The local Matakanui Combined Club, based in Ōmakau, has been very successful over the years, but fair to say it's fallen on tough times lately. Still, I'd watch 'The Mudfish' every weekend if I could. Rugby may not draw as many people out of the woods as it used to, but in a tight-knit little community like ours, it's still easily the best social catch-up of the week. I'd happily hit 'the bank' with the kids, or go alone in the early afternoon, just in time for kick-off. If the children were with me, I'd invariably lose them within seconds of arriving. They'd be playing their own 'test matches' down the sideline for the rest of the day.

At matches it's often sunny, and it's hard to beat having the sun on your face. Before the game gets under way there's a wee window for a chat to Bill or Graeme or Cam or Paddy or Dave or Adam. They're all keen to throw a bit of shit at me; all keen on having a laugh. It's the best medicine. Then the players start lining up, the whistle's about to blow, the smell of liniment fills the air. It takes me back to South Otago and the 1980s. Back to happy days. I briefly watch the kids playing between the embankment fence and the sideline. They're ripping into it. Running. Tackling. Smiling. Laughing. In that moment, everyone looks like they're living their best life.

Gary, the referee, blows his whistle and it's game on. Our boys, in red and green, might lack a bit of finesse but they play with so much heart. It's not easy for the farmers and a few tradies to take on the flash teams from Queenstown and Wānaka, who have so many more players to pick from; but up front, at least, they match 'em. And while Deano, Stumpy, Porter and the others are giving it everything they've got out on the track, I'm pacing up and down the sideline looking like a bloke who has just escaped some kind of mental asylum. Yelling, 'C'mon Matak . . . Big scrum — take it off 'em'. I just have to follow the game. Have to get right up close to the action. Later, a friend tells me that two different people asked her if I was the manager of the team.

Gary, the referee, blows his whistle and it's game on. Our boys, in red and green, might lack a bit of finesse but they play with so much heart.

Of course I'm not, but I do take it really seriously. Sometimes I even consider myself a part of the team. I go to the odd training sesh. I talk to a lot of the players. And I've dished out a few fines at a court session. Matakanui are often on attack for big chunks of the game, but then lose the ball and end up watching the often quicker opposition run 70, 80 or 90 metres and score at the other end of the field. We call 'em 14-point tries. It's a little heart-breaking, but we're used to it. After the final whistle, Matakanui often ends up with fewer points than the other team.

I usually go and thank the lads for giving it their all, for giving me the best entertainment I've had all week. Then we stand around chatting. The sun's still shining. 'We've' lost, but we're still winning. Life goes on. It's either home to help with the kids, or into the clubrooms for a couple of cold ones and a few more catch-ups. If the kids are with me, none of us want to go home. None of us want that afternoon to end. The boys and I have been known to arrive home at ten o'clock at night, well after bed-time, covered in mud from the afternoon's 'test match', and slip into bed without a bath.

So, rugby's always been my game. I never considered even for a moment that my boys would want to play soccer, or what I'm told is more correctly called football. Especially considering that in the Manuherikia and Ida valleys, they've never played 'football' for the hundreds of years people have lived here. This is rugby country. If I'd played soccer as a schoolboy growing up in South Otago, not too far away from here, in the 1980s I would have been bullied from nine in the morning till three in the afternoon. 'Ya bloody soccer poof.' 'Ya faggot.' 'Ya bloody girl.' The abuse would have been incessant. I can't quite remember, but being a rugby-mad whippersnapper back in the day I probably hurled some of that abuse myself. Luckily both Bede and Finn were pretty set on playing 'ripper rugby'.

Change, though, can be a really good thing, even if it is a little scary at first. One day, Bede and Finn come home from school and say, 'Dad, we're going to play football.' I quickly reply, 'Like bloody hell you are. And you can't, anyway — you've got rugby.' Bede, though, at just six, is almost quicker than his old man with the come-backs nowadays. 'No, Dad, we'll play ripper on a Saturday, and football on a Sunday.' I was stumped. It was either 'screen-time Sundays' or take 'em to soccer, and even though soccer could mean a 200-kilometre round trip every weekend, soccer won. A week later Bede was in the first-ever Ōmakau Under 7 football team, Finn

Opposite top Shouting instructions on the field at ripper rugby.

Opposite Some post-match analysis with Deano (Dean Sinnamon) from the men's team.

was in the first-ever Ōmakau Under 6 team, and after the first training — even though I didn't have a bloody clue — I was the coach.

Living at Ōmakau, we were across the road from the Hintons: Kyle, Kelsey and their three boys, Oakley, Brock and Cruze. Those boys are very talented wee sportspeople. The Hintons would have to be some of the most community-minded people you could meet. If there's something on, the Hintons have helped organise it and are there, with their sleeves rolled up, getting amongst it. Kyle, a carpet layer, is also sports-mad. His living room TV probably wouldn't be out of place on the wall at Alexandra's movie theatre and I reckon when he's watching telly, nine times out of ten he's watching sport. Apparently, he was pretty handy in his day, too.

Kyle's the kind of dad who's always out on the vacant section with the kids, throwing the rugby ball, kicking the football, bowling the cricket ball until you can't see the ball anymore because it's too dark. He's the kind of dad who gets the whole village involved. Anyway, even though Oakley (then seven) and Brock (six) played organised rugby every weekend, they must've wanted to play football as well. They could've made the 45-minute round trip in and out of Alexandra to play for the thriving Alex club, like a few families were already doing, but Kyle had other ideas. Kids started talking at school, their parents started receiving Facebook messages, and Kyle started writing team lists. After he'd had a few chats with the top brass of that Alexandra club, 'Ōmakau' would field two teams in the Alex colours but would train at Omakau school. The old-timers buried right beside that school would have been turning in their graves every Friday afternoon as Kyle and I took our practices.

I don't think I was meant to be the coach of the Under 6 side; I think the parents were going to share the role. I would never have put my hand up because (1) I didn't really know anything about the game, and (2) I'm away out of the area working a lot. Anyway, I seem to recall taking my turn as coach for the first training and the first game, but I enjoyed it so much

Opposite Kyle Hinton and his boys.

WSH
M
MATAKANUI
SPORTS

I didn't want to give the job up. 'Coaching' or cajoling, or just pointing those kids in the right direction, was a bit of a life-saver for me back then. For a couple of days each week I wasn't concerned about the cost-of-living crisis, or my mortgage, or my budget, or food security, I was right there, on the field, with those wee five-year-olds. In the moment, up close, as they saved a goal, or scored one, watching the delight on their little faces when they surprised themselves with their ability. I might've been tired and grumpy while driving the kids to those games, but as soon as we were out of the ute and kicking the football around, it was almost like I was using a drug all over again and didn't want to stop using it. I'd be disappointed when the first game was over, but delighted when I realised there were still five more games to come that day.

The kids' football soon became one of the coolest little chapters of my life. The primarily farm kids from the Manuherikia and Ida valleys played against kids from the bigger, and arguably flasher, towns like Alex, Cromwell, Arrowtown, Queenstown and Wānaka. Early on, at least with the Under 7s, we were cleaning them up. They were like the ice-hockey kids in *The Mighty Ducks* movie and there was an amazing buzz around the teams. Elle and I were getting to know all of the kids and their parents, and it really felt like we were a small part of something really special. It didn't take long before other people realised just how special the first season of football in Ōmakau was, either. A former colleague of mine saw a social media post I did, and next minute *1News* was in town and our wee kids were on the telly. People messaged me and told me how they loved the vibe of our teams and appreciated the enthusiasm I brought to the game. Random people approached me on the field and told me the same thing.

The kids' football soon became one of the coolest little chapters of my life.

Not everyone was impressed, though. One Sunday morning we were playing on what would have to be one of the most picturesque pitches on the planet, at the foot of the Remarkables, in Queenstown. Our wee Ōmakau Under 6 team had a good first game and were set to play a Cromwell side next. Usually our kids would play three 10-minute games in about 45 minutes, so there's no mucking around. After a game, the coach has to find the next opposition team and the field you'll be playing on in about five minutes before kick-off. On this particular day, it wasn't hard to spot the coach of the Cromwell team. With a whistle around his neck and a clipboard in his hand, he was running scoring drills with his wee five-year-olds. I approached him.

'G'day, Matt from Ōmakau — have you got four players?'

'Yep.'

'Great, we're kicking off on field three over here in about a minute.'

The game starts, and everyone behaves as they usually do. Our best player, Izzy from the Maniototo, starts carving up the opposition. My wee fella, Finn, is determined on defence, but unhappy with a couple of his old man's calls. Will is trapping and dribbling beautifully. Fletcher and Marlo appear to be playing their own game within the game. Might be a game of tag. The Cromwell players are likewise doing their thing. Like me, the Cromwell coach is also very vocal and passionate, encouraging his wee chargers. The ball goes out across the line, but I don't see who the ball comes off so I ask the spectators. Without realising it, I've upset the opposition coach. We're just two minutes into the game. I gather the ball, place it on the line, look up — and the opposition coach is standing over me, right in my face. Finding the situation hard to believe, thinking maybe this is some kind of *Candid Camera* moment, I don't take in the first thing he says to me — but I fully understand the second. 'You're intimidating our children,' he says.

Now, I know I shouldn't have, but in disbelief I respond: 'What the fuck?' He carries on telling me that I'm intimidating his players even though he clearly hasn't had a conversation with them. I'm not known for fighting, but this is a situation that's going to go either one of two ways. I eventually tell him to fuck off — he's seeing things that aren't there. If I

TRADE MARK

ever thought I was capable of intimidating children, I wouldn't get out of bed of a morning.

Within a minute there's about four different adults on the field trying to defuse the situation — a situation I've never found myself in before. The opposition coach now wants us to both leave the field. The parents of my wee five-year-olds tell me to stand my ground. To stay on the field. They tell me their kids need me. And then, while one of those wee kids is dribbling down the field, the opposition coach actually bends over and traps the ball. He's completely lost the plot. A minute later, a spectator from Cromwell who's had his ear chewed off by the Cromwell coach accuses me of cheating. He accuses me of standing in the goal to stop the opposition kids from scoring goals.

Remember, we're talking about *five-year-old kids* here. You seriously couldn't make this stuff up. The game is called off early. It's one of the most hideous little pockets of time I've ever been involved in. My head is racing. Is there any truth to what this guy is saying? Is my big, enthusiastic, encouraging personality actually intimidating children?

I tell the kids' parents I'm done; I don't want to coach anymore. I tell them I don't ever want to be in this situation again. They continue saying all the right things — that it's not about me, it's about this other 'muppet'.

As everyone begins leaving, I recognise a bigwig from the Cromwell club. He's a guy who's watched me coach before. I approach him and explain exactly what's just gone down while it's still fresh in my mind. And even though there could be a handful of Cromwell Under 6 coaches, he immediately picks the one that was involved — and he encourages me to continue coaching. 'Don't let this guy put you off. I've enjoyed watching you with those wee kids, and you're just what the sport needs.'

I'm not convinced as I traipse over the fields back to the ute. Where I find a nice little surprise: a classic little coffee cup, with a sheep drawn on it along with a handwritten message from one of the kids' parents. 'Matt, you're flocking awesome and our little flock really needs you.' It got me welling up. Our new little Ōmakau football community couldn't have been any cooler or more supportive. Still, the hour-long drive home wasn't good for my overthinking mind.

Later that night, I got a call from Kyle. 'Mate, how you feeling? I don't want you to worry about anything. The Cromwell team have laid a complaint against you, but I've talked to the guys from both the Alexandra and Cromwell clubs, who both think you're awesome, and it's not going to go any further. Don't let this idiot put you off.' Elle backed Kyle up. 'You didn't do anything wrong. Every other bloke around here would have reacted the same way you did.'

Although I really disliked the fact that I'd got involved in a hideous kids' sport moment like that, I was eventually convinced that I shouldn't throw the towel in — and I'm so pleased I didn't. Coaching that Under 6 soccer team has been one of the best things I've ever done in my life. It's gone a long way in helping to get me out of my head and be present.

JUST WEEKS AFTER KYLE KICK-STARTED kids' football in the area, he somehow managed to get a men's team together, too. A few waifs and strays and a whole lot of forty-something, washed-up rugby players and farmers took on a Cromwell 'B' team one sunny Saturday afternoon. I'm pretty sure that this was the first time men from the area had played a competitive game of football.

Twenty years after hanging up my rugby boots, at the tender age of 46 I made my football debut. We got a hiding, but it didn't matter. I had forgotten just how good the endorphin- and camaraderie-filled cocktail of team sport was. Most of us were immediately hooked. Not long after that Cromwell game, we lined up against the competition-leading Alexandra 'B' side. Without even having a training run, our ragtag 'Manuherikia United' — our own Man U — team was somehow 1–nil up after just a few minutes. Sure most of us had never played the game before, but we'd played a lot of sport and were all pretty bloody determined. We weren't winning for long, though. After 30 minutes, Alex brought on an entirely new team; we had one sub. I think we went down 6–2 in the end.

I went to a couple of trainings after that game and really enjoyed them, but had to pull the pin on my football season before the end of the year. Even though football was so good for me on so many different levels, I just didn't have the time to do enough work to pay the mortgage, run a small farm, be a good dad, write this book *and* play football. I had learnt enough, though, to know that football really is a beautiful game and that I'll lace up my new soccer boots again next season. I'm bloody sure the boys will, too. They don't stop talking about Messi, Ronaldo, Neymar and Mbappé. In fact, they asked me so many questions about football that I couldn't answer that I was constantly googling. Then, I turned the telly on. By then the telly had been turned off for so long that when I turned it on, I could barely remember how to use it. I managed, though, and we all stayed up far too late watching the women's football World Cup on home soil. One Friday I took a day off work and jumped on a bus with some Omakau School students, organised by Southern Football, and went through to Dunedin to watch Argentina play South Africa. Two days later, Elle and I drove the family back through to Dunedin again to watch our Football Ferns take on Switzerland.

I didn't want to miss a minute of that World Cup. I reckon that one of the best things about life — if you're lucky enough to live long enough — is that you can constantly reinvent yourself. Life isn't necessarily black and white. With some maturity, you can actually like rugby *and* football.

The day in between those two football matches in Dunedin, I took the boys to a rugby tournament in Millers Flat, near Roxburgh. I'd played in that tournament 40 years earlier. Change can be nice, but it's also nice when some things stay the same.

AUFC
TRADE MA
CENTRAL

DREAM HOME

While we ventured south for a quieter life, in fact we've never been so busy. No point fighting it, though — sometimes you just have to accept what is and get on with it.

We built our dream home during the Covid-19 pandemic — a time when half the world wasn't working, when building materials became a whole lot more scarce and expensive. As you'll recall, Elle and I had been talking about living our dream for half a dozen years before we took the plunge, and building our dream home was always going to be a big part of that plan. We had 'concept drawings' drawn up about five years before we started building. I remember taking breaks from learning lines while filming *Survivor New Zealand* in Thailand in 2018 to look at plans our designer had drawn up.

I also remember spitting tacks on that same trip when a quantity surveyor costed out those plans and reckoned the house we wanted to build would cost about 40% more than we wanted to spend. Our Dunedin-based designer said, 'Look, you don't need to freak out — these costings will be based on a Wānaka or Queenstown build. What you need

Opposite Working on the lawn with Dave Cockburn.

to do is find a good local builder, who'll look after you.' He was right. There was a good local builder in our valley and he was a stand-up bloke. Dave Cockburn had built Elle's parents' and sister and brother-in-law's houses and they couldn't say a bad word about him.

After pulling a few non-essential items out of the build, we sent Dave the plans, and he priced them up and reckoned he could build it on our budget. The problem was, we weren't yet ready to build. We were still in Auckland; we needed to move south and we needed to sell those 15 acres before we could start, and that took a couple of years to do. By the time we were ready to pull the trigger, things had changed. Dave called, saying something like, 'Matty, we've had to reprice the house — prices have gone through the roof. Steel's up around 33%, concrete's up 25, roofing's up like 40. Sorry, mate, but there's no way we'll be able to build your house for what we initially said without losing a lot of money.'

> **I kept telling myself two things: 'there's never a better time to build than now' and 'we're only ever going to build one house on our land'.**

I'd been listening to the news and reading the websites, and knew this call was coming. I was actually surprised when the new price for the build came in only about 15% higher than the initial one. Now, I reckon a lot of people tried it on during the pandemic — took advantage and made a lot of money. Dave's not one of those people. At that stage — even at the new build price — our monthly mortgage payments weren't going to be considerably more than our rent, so we boxed on. After kicking around concepts and plans for a few years, we definitely didn't want to go back to the drawing board now.

As it happened, we waited and waited for the designer to deliver our plans to council, worrying as he missed deadline after deadline — and prices kept on going up. I kept telling myself two things: 'there's never a better time to build than now' and 'we're only ever going to build one house on our land'. And the house we wanted to build wasn't *really* flash. Sure, it was bigger than your average house, made from nice materials and it was going to be warm, because when you're building in one of the coldest places in the country you need to build a warm house. It needed to be reasonably big because as a family of five, with big personalities, we needed to be able to get away from each other at times. We also wanted to make the most of our phenomenal views. We wanted to be able to look south down to Alexandra, the Raggedys and the Old Man Range, west to the Dunstans and north to Elle's parents' Magdalen hills. So our minimalistic mono-pitch steel-and-cedar home had huge windows, and glass doors off our living room.

We eventually got both the green light to build and tradies who were ready to rip into it.

AFTER OUR REALLY LONG WAIT, the build was always going to be exciting. My skill-set is pretty much confined to talking, so I think builders are magicians — amazing how they can turn a paddock into a palace. Since our Chatto Creek house was just five minutes down the road from Ōmakau, every day I was home I'd poke my head in for a look on my way down to 'The Land' to do my farming. Brad, at just 23, was running the job and he was a star. I marvelled at how he speedily solved problems and put all the pieces of the puzzle together. I enjoyed bantering with the builders and would try to reward them for their hard work with a box of beers most Fridays. For a person who doesn't drink, I buy a lot of alcohol. Giving someone a box of beer is a pretty common way of saying 'thank you' in the country.

Most nights, once the kids were in bed I'd head back down to 'The Land' and walk around the site in the dark, using the light on my phone to track the tradies' progress. I'd appreciate the changing shape of the structure. The clean lines. The spaces. I'd think about who was going to fill those spaces and the moments we'd create in them. I was always very

mindful; always very grateful. Appreciating the whole thing coming together; the centrepiece of our little slice of paradise.

Building is always a busy time. It's also an expensive one. You're forever fielding questions and being asked if you'd like to spend more money. 'We've allowed for this-sized heat pump in the living room, but it's not going to be big enough to do the job. You'll need one twice the size, which will cost you another 1,500 bucks.'

Everything seemed to be another 1,500 bucks. Nine times out of ten we agreed to spend the extra money, because 'we're only ever going to build one house on our land'. As we didn't have a fixed-price contract and the prices kept going up while we were building, we had to pay for the increase. When each stage was completed we'd make another progress payment — first using money we had in the bank after selling that land, then using money we borrowed from the bank. And when we were getting close to the end of the job, I realised we'd have to borrow some *more* money, so we did. In the end we borrowed a couple of hundred thousand dollars more than we wanted to borrow. By this time, with inflationary pressure off the back of the pandemic, we were watching the Reserve Bank raise the official cash rate and therefore interest rates what seemed like every five minutes. Before we started the build, the bank's online mortgage calculator had suggested I'd need to earn $80,000 a year to pay our mortgage and be able to live. Now, I needed to earn about that $80,000 just to pay our mortgage.

The uncertainty around that pandemic was also really stressful. It was hard to know just what our income was going to be. Would we film TV shows or not? Our first year out of Auckland, we didn't film *Celebrity Treasure Island*. In the second year we did film the show, but didn't really know it was actually going to happen until filming started. That meant I didn't know whether or not I'd have that income until I had the income. Once we started filming the show, which was always a bit of a slog, I started shopping — probably to make myself feel better — without really thinking too much about our financial future.

Back in 2014, before we'd bought land, but knowing we'd end up on some dirt one day, Elle and I bought a brand-new Toyota Hilux ute. It was our pride and joy (there were no children on the ground yet). Shit, we even gave it a name — Angus — because it was black like Angus cattle. Early on, I kept baby Angus spic and span and when the kids arrived it became our family vehicle. When we moved south, that family vehicle also became the farm ute and it was getting a real hiding. We don't need much rain here for vehicles to start sliding all over the show, and one day I sped through a muddy gateway and, in what felt like slow motion, slid into a fence-post, scratching the bejesus out of about four panels. Shortly afterwards, while I was chasing stock and trying to cut them off, I backed into a fence at speed and mangled the bumper. Fortunately, we were insured, so I put in two claims at once.

The inside of the ute was probably worse than the outside. Depending on the time of year, it would be full of drench and dip, or lamb covers and tags and taggers, or string, or plastic bale wrap that'd blown over to ours from the neighbours. No matter what time of year, there'd be a dozen takeaway coffee cups, half a dozen pie wrappers, and empty packets of chips and liquorice. Once, arguably, a status symbol and something to be proud of, Angus was now merely a tool and Elle and I wanted to get a new (to us) vehicle for the farm. I'd been looking at old flat-deck Hiluxes on Trade Me for months, and as soon as I knew for sure that *Treasure Island* was going ahead, I felt okay about buying one, even though we were dropping all that money on a new house.

One night after filming, and after I had my reality TV lines for the next day cemented in my head, I jumped on the net and found a new listing — a red 1999 Toyota Hilux ute with just 100,000 k on the clock. We'd done more in Angus. This machine was bloody nearly a collector's item and it was only about an hour and a half down the road in Edievale. I called the owner, believed him when he said the mileage was genuine, got the good oil from someone from the garage who'd been servicing the old girl, and — feeling like I'd done my due diligence — transferred the money.

That wasn't the only big purchase I made for the farm on that work trip. I also spent nearly $5,000 on a purebred Swiss Valais Blacknose ram. Having used just a three-quarter Valais ram the previous season, and thinking 'we're a long time dead', I reckoned I should go all the way. I also made a huge investment in my stud Southdown flock. I'd already spent more than $2,000 on 'JJ' at Dave Robertson's Ōamaru sale, but had my heart set on some more of Blair Robertson's ewes. After my first Merrydowns ewes had performed so well — remember I got eleven great lambs from just six ewes in 2020 — I wanted more. Blair hadn't wanted to sell me any the following year, but for some reason he changed his mind for the 2022 season, and I paid through the nose for 24 mixed-age Merrydowns Southdown ewes. I had a good ram, so surely it made sense to nab a few more ewes. I always wondered how I'd get on if I had a whole lot more sheep; well, a whole lot more sheep for me. I could easily sell five or six Southdown rams a year, but could I sell, say, twenty? Plus, what sort of a breeder has only ten ewes?

Either way, by the time I'd bought the red ute, 24 ewes and a ram, I'd spent a bloody good chunk of my *Treasure Island* income. In hindsight, maybe I shouldn't have spent all that money on my hobby in the middle of building our dream home, but I was going through a really good patch mentally and felt kind of untouchable. I felt like everything was going to work out.

Now, while the world was meant to be going green, we had two diesel-burning Toyota Hilux utes. The 2014 double-cab was now supposed to be the family wagon again, and the new-but-old 1999 flat-deck was supposed to be my farm vehicle. Anyhow, one night when the boys and I were going for a cruise in the flat-deck we discovered that both of our Highland cows had horns that were growing into one side of their faces. We had to get the vet in and dehorn them before we had an issue. I lined up the vet, but on the day before the job was to be done I got a call from Dennis: 'Look, I'm having a bit of trouble with my ute, can I borrow your wee red one for a bit?' You'd never say no in a situation like that.

So with Dennis off in our red ute, I was back in the black one to yard the Highland cows. Those cows were running with the rest of the herd, and I wanted to 'cut them out' of that herd so I didn't need to take all twenty cows all the way to Dennis's yards. Using the ute, I'd isolate the two I wanted, then chase them to the yards. Most of the time, animals don't want to be cut off from their paddock mates. They'll often try to dart back to them, but after a while they give up trying and are a little more obliging. Now, I don't know whether or not Ginger Nut and Creamy Milk knew why they were going to the yards, but they really didn't want to get cut out of the herd. I can't even remember which bloody cow it was now, but one of them was rampaging back, along the fence-line, to join the cattle I didn't want, so I reversed back to block her path. Between the ute and the fence, she'd have nowhere to go. Angry, and this time beaten after what had probably already been a five-minute game of cat and mouse, she took a massive swipe with her head and those horns — the ones that were about to be taken off it — dented and scraped across about five panels. At this point, she was well and truly winning the game. And, giving her more points, it wasn't the old overpriced red ute that got a hiding that day, but the family wagon.

I was steaming, and I *still* had to yard those two cows because the vet was on his way. Eventually I got the job done. While the animal doctor was keen to give that cow some anaesthetic for the pain before we whipped off her horns, I had a moment when I wasn't so sure. If that cow was ever actually going to have a calf, any profit I made would already have gone on the insurance excess for the ute.

About a year after the damage was done, the ute still hadn't been fixed. I kept telling myself: 'I'll get that done when I have time.' We don't have a lot of time. Or money.

JULY THE 10TH, 2022 WAS a special day. I'd spent my entire life wanting to live in a house on a small farm, and this was the day we actually started moving into a house on a small farm. Our dream home on 'The Land'. Having planned, schemed, plotted and agonised over the move for years, finally it was happening.

Moving house is never a lot of fun, but once we were done we could relax and enjoy it. We didn't know ourselves. Our trusty local builder Dave Cockburn and his team had done an amazing job. Including the garage, our long, spacious farm house was nearly three times the size of our wee Ōmakau rental. We had so much space. And we no longer had to drive down the road to the farm to enjoy those phenomenal views — they were right there out the window. We could appreciate them over dinner and when we woke each morning. Elle and I both felt incredibly grateful. Incredibly lucky.

However, I reckon a wee switch in my brain got flicked that day. I immediately started worrying about losing it all. Losing our dream home on our dream bit of dirt. While we were now living in our beautiful new home, right where we wanted to be, we still had so much to do. There was the lawns, the landscaping, the fencing, not to mention the farming, and we could only start thinking about doing all those things *after* we'd met our large mortgage repayments.

I CAN'T REMEMBER EXACTLY WHEN it happened, but not too long after going country I stopped watching television. I think this happened for a few different reasons. First, I really didn't have much time so wanted to spend the limited spare time I *did* have doing things that filled my cup. That usually meant being out on the land. I also found the telly far too negative and, at times, triggering. Just a few seconds of the box could put me in a bit of a spin. I didn't want to know who was hosting this, or who was working on that, so I often had to turn the telly off or leave the room. I had moved on from that world and generally felt better for it.

But there was a problem. If I wasn't watching the telly, if I wasn't following current affairs or closely following *Country Calendar*, how could

I actually make current affairs shows or put *Country Calendar* stories together? Also, being technologically illiterate, I had trouble viewing footage and writing scripts from home. I lost whole days simply trying to get into the right systems. I was also becoming too busy — I didn't have time to do all the work that was coming my way. Plus, *Sunday* had pulled the pin on my contract, so I was no longer guaranteed a certain number of stories a year. It would have been hard for me to pitch stories to a producer when I'd stopped really following what was happening in the world. When *Country Calendar* wanted me to go back and finish filming a story that had been cut short because of Covid, I had other things on. It all got a little bit too hard; and I actually didn't want to do that kind of work anymore. I might well have burnt some bridges at TVNZ by not explaining my thinking clearly at the time, but life goes on.

A couple of years before I left the Auckland newsroom, the lovely soundy Graham Wallace sidled up to my desk for a chat. 'Matt, where did you say your bit of dirt was down south?'

'Chatto Creek, Graham — population about 50.'

'Amazing,' he replied. 'I'm pretty sure that's where Scotty and Suzy Lee have bought.'

Suzy does hair and make-up for movies that are filmed down under, and Scotty is a world-class cameraman who I'd worked with once filming promos for *Close Up*. While I'd never met Suzy, I could picture Scotty's cheeky face and remembered him being very funny. People who work behind the camera are often funnier than the people in front of it.

What a small world it can be sometimes. Graham was right — almost unbelievably, Suzy, Scotty and their two boys, Nico and Louis, lived on 25 acres at Chatto Creek, only about a cricket-ball throw away from us. Once we'd shifted down to Ōmakau it didn't take long for us all to become great friends. Bede and Louis are just three months apart and bloody near inseparable. Finn tags along — sometimes they all get along; sometimes there're dust-ups. Nico is brilliant with Bree, Suzy and Elle are besties, and Scotty and I have become great cobbers.

Scotty is the kind of guy who is so competent and talented that he almost pisses you off. He's a phenomenal cook, does his own farm fencing, and he's even built his own shed. An 84-square-metre timber-and-iron shed. While I'd spend months trying to build a mailbox and still wouldn't have it finished, Scotty has single-handedly put together a shed big enough to house two or three tractors or a whole lot of smaller sheds. The guy is a bloody genius. Though of all the people in our area, no one has a more similar back story, sense of humour, or outlook on life than me and Scotty.

We kept bumping into each other at the kids' school, or the store, or the river, but our mateship really grew on the job. We teamed up to film a few episodes of something called *Country Living* for the Allied Press, who own the *Otago Daily Times*, but really cemented our bromance filming *Nadia's Farm* for Warner Brothers and TV3. I'd first met TV producer Tim Lawry back in 2016 when he auditioned me to host *Survivor New Zealand.* Surprisingly (for me at least), I got the gig and Tim and I would work together on four seasons of reality TV: two seasons of *Survivor* and two seasons of *Celebrity Treasure Island*. When we finally moved south, Tim asked whether I'd be interested in producing Nadia Lim's farm show. It was a no-brainer. I like making TV with good people, love talking farming and knew that Nadia was a good stick, having interviewed her before. So when Tim asked if I knew of a good local cameraman, I didn't have to look far. Actually, I just had to look out of the kitchen window.

Scotty and I must have filmed about 70 days of content at Nadia Lim and Carlos Bagrie's Royalburn Station, and every single one of those days was a day well spent. First, it takes about an hour for the pair of us to get to the Crown Terrace property and (funnily enough) about an hour to get home. That typically means Scotty and me kicking around anything from farming to footy to our wives to the kids to cooking or to the epic little community we live in. We dream about being debt-free, and what we'll do with all our spare time when we're out of the trenches. We laugh. We laugh so much that if other people were to hear us, they'd probably wonder whether we were on some sort of drug. Once we're at Royalburn, our time there is just as good. Nadia and Carlos are great people who actually share a reasonably similar sense of humour to Scotty and me. I reckon people make the best content when everyone is on the same page, and we're all on the same page at Royalburn. And when I say everyone, I'm also talking about the twenty-odd people who work there. We're all interested in farming and food and fun. The vibe is usually so good that it doesn't feel like work. We're all learning, too, and hopefully educating others at the same time.

It's a privilege to play a small part in *Nadia's Farm*, but for a while there it was also tough going. Although we're working directly with Nadia, Carlos and their team, we're actually contracted to Warner Brothers New Zealand, the production company who've made the reality TV shows I've hosted — *Survivor New Zealand* and *Celebrity Treasure Island*. As mentioned earlier, I hosted four of those shows under Tim Lawry, who was also heading up *Nadia's Farm*, but Tim didn't produce the last season of *Treasure Island* I was involved in. Now, that last season of *CTI* was bloody hard. Initially, because of the Covid-19 lockdowns, we weren't even sure we'd film the 2022 season until the last minute. And, remember, we were still building our dream home and I really needed the income from the show. Then, while we were preparing to film on location in the far north, participant Va'aiga Tuigamala died, aged just 52.

There was a hell of a lot going on, and we had a new boss at the helm calling the shots. Right off the bat, I struggled with the way this new boss talked to me. I struggled with her tone and what seemed like a lack of respect. When I tried to talk to her about whether we could do some things better, our relationship became worse. Even though I'd been hosting those shows for several seasons, it seemed like I couldn't have an opinion on anything. In the end, I gave up trying to make things better for the overall production and focused on what I could control: my performance.

I came away from that work trip expecting a big debrief about what

Opposite Having a laugh with Scotty Lee.

SANTA CRUZ

went on while filming the show, but it never came. About four months later, though, I received a call from one of the big bosses. 'Matt, we're not going to take you on the next season of *Celebrity Treasure Island*. You obviously don't get on with the new boss, and we know you don't enjoy it — you've written about not enjoying it in your book.' I'd also written about how I'd learnt to enjoy filming those shows, but it didn't matter, I was gone. After hosting those shows for seven years.

I pride myself on my ability to get on with people, but now I'd lost my biggest source of income because I didn't get on with someone.

While it wasn't always easy working for Warner Brothers on *Nadia's Farm*, I always tried to focus on the many positives and just get on with it.

Later, when *Celebrity Treasure Island* was about to air, journalists wanted to know why I wasn't at the launch party. They'd got wind of the fact that I wasn't hosting the next season and wanted to run a story. I didn't want to talk to them. Someone from TVNZ told me that I could 'control the narrative'. They told me — a journalist who relies on credibility to do my job — that I could lie to our viewers, the people who had watched me on TV for the past fifteen years, and tell them I'd decided to stand down from the show to spend more time with my family. I wasn't for one moment going to tell anyone that, because that wasn't what happened.

I didn't watch one second of the final season of *Celebrity Treasure Island* that I hosted. I also had to stop following my co-host and great mate Bree Tomasel on social media. Not her fault, but it was all far too triggering for me.

Some time earlier, Tim Lawry had sent me an email. He'd said something really nice about my hosting ability, but — more importantly to me — that I always did the right thing in any situation. It's amazing how just one person can make you or break you.

Instead of washing my hands of that chapter of my life, I should celebrate it. That chapter has allowed me to live this new chapter — and this one is fantastic. I have an amazing photo of me on a beach, hosting *Celebrity Treasure Island*, with former All Blacks captain Buck Shelford up a pole hanging on for dear life, and about a dozen cameras in shot. That's me living one of my childhood dreams. It should be celebrated, not forgotten. I'm going to frame that photo to remind me and others to keep pushing, to keep chasing dreams.

Nowadays, I'm either farming or filming at Nadia Lim's farm, or interviewing someone for a speech, writing a speech, driving or flying to deliver a speech, delivering a speech, driving or flying home from delivering a speech, or invoicing someone for a speech. I don't mind the driving, hate the flying, and really enjoy the public speaking. I thrive on the immediate feedback, making people laugh, and making them feel something. While I don't really like saying it, or writing it down, I've come to think I'm reasonably good at public speaking.

IT'S NICE WORKING FOR A salary, but you don't fully appreciate it until you're no longer getting one. Nowadays, I'm always more worried about organising work and then doing the work than I am about invoicing for the work. I don't like admin; never have, never will. Anyway, towards the end of our build I'd been working pretty hard all over the country and it had been a while since I'd been paid, because it had been a while since I had done any invoicing. And one day, when I was in Wellington Airport on my way home from Fieldays at Mystery Creek, my card was declined ordering a $5.50 coffee. It was embarrassing. Almost like being back at Lincoln University in the '90s with my card being declined at the bar — only now I was sober, had grey hair, and wasn't used to having my card declined. Thinking that we should have about ten grand up our sleeves, I quickly checked the accounts. Elle had paid a whole lot of big bills, and then, at the end of the month, our mortgage went out. It meant that one of our accounts was overdrawn, so I transferred some money to cover it. My credit card was tapped out as well, and now, no matter what I did, I couldn't rustle up enough dough for a cuppa. I was pissed off, but hadn't thrown my toys just yet. Caffeine's pretty much the only drug I use nowadays and I quite like it, but was happy enough with the basic one I was given on the flight into Queenstown.

At this point it all turns to custard. Off the plane, keys out of the bag, parking ticket out of the wallet — shit! I can't pay for the parking, and if I can't pay for the parking then I can't leave the airport car park. By this stage Elle has transferred some money across to me, but it hasn't shown up yet. It's three o'clock on a Saturday afternoon. I've been away for days, and I'm tired and I'm hungry and all I want to do is *get home*. But I can't. Pacing around this car park I can't escape, I ring my bank. I listen to hold music for half an hour. It's not really the playlist I'd choose, and I'm starting to get really pissed off. Eventually I'm able to talk to someone, but her 'hands are tied'. While I think it's fine for her to slip a couple of hundred bucks into my account, because 'I'm good for it — I've got thirty or forty grand owing to me', she works for a bank and wants me to fill in a whole lot of forms, which people will look at next week. The phone conversation goes on for a while, but it isn't going anywhere fast and I am really losing it and that is really obvious.

A bloke who's walked past a few times, carrying crates of milk, stops and asks if I am okay. I end what was probably always going to be a futile conversation, and explain my plight to him. Warwick knows who I am — he's heard me speak — and wants to help. 'Mate, how much do you need? 200? 500?'

Within five minutes Warwick has handed me $200 that he has taken out of an airport ATM, and in doing that he saves my arse; he allows me to get home.

Days later, when I asked for his bank account details, he replied, 'Slap that coin into the charity you represent.' But even though he didn't want it, I made sure Warwick from Wakatipu got his money back. What a good bastard.

MORE GOOD BASTARDS

It can get bloody dry here. You can almost see the land burning up in front of you; almost see the wind ripping the moisture out of the ground. It can actually blow so hard that if you're working outside you have to pull the pin, and find a job inside. I always notice the difference coming home after being away for a few days. People say we're always just two weeks of wind away from a drought. Of course, those horrifically hot summers make Central Otago a magnet for holidaymakers, but it can be a terribly cruel place to farm. If you haven't got water, you're all but pissing into the wind.

Now, I've never been known for my forward planning, which I'm beginning to think is what farming is all about. As well as that, being just a part-timer, my paid work always comes first, and that means I don't always get the farm jobs done when they need to be done. Watering the dry-as-an-old-chip dirt was a good example of that.

Back in 2015, when we bought our first bit of dirt, we also bought thousands of dollars worth of 'k-line'. If you're borrowing nearly quarter of

Previous spread Time for a yarn with Scotty Lee.

Opposite Our trusty local builder Dave Cockburn.

a million dollars, what's another fifteen thou? K-line is essentially a heap of sprinklers, inside pods spread out at equal distances from each other on a piece of long pipe lying on top of the ground. I don't know why we bought all those sprinklers, pods and pipes when we did, because we were still living in Auckland, but we did and it gathered dust in a shed for half a dozen years. It also played on my mind.

As usual, in the summer of 2021/2022 we got really dry. I talked to our neighbour, Robbo, who sometimes works with a fella setting up k-line irrigation. He's called 'One-Armed Wally' because he's only got one arm. Robbo gave me One-Armed Wally's number and I gave him a call. He was flat-out for months, which wasn't going to work for me. I was desperate: if I couldn't throw some water around I couldn't grow any tucker, and I couldn't feed my animals. Simple as that.

One day in Alexandra I ran into a bloke who worked for a business that sold irrigation equipment. Naturally he was keen to sell me the extra bits and pieces I needed to get me up and running. I still had the problem, though, of putting it all together. Not only was it something I'd never done before, but — as always — I didn't have much time to do it and there was no one available to do it for me for several weeks.

Then Elle remembered that a good mate of hers, who'd just moved into the valley, worked for the same irrigation company as the bloke I'd met in Alexandra. I reached out to this guy, Adam Hildebrand, who said something like: 'I'm bloody busy, Horse, but I'm happy to help you get started, eh.'

Adam, who's from Bluff, went to Verdon College, in Invercargill, at the same time as Elle. He's a handsome young fella who probably doesn't know how handsome he is. Adam doesn't spend tonnes of time talking, but when he does talk he's well worth listening to. A hard-working bloke with good morals, who keeps life fairly simple.

In what was his busiest time of the year, Adam gave me something

Opposite Adam Hildebrand with his dog, Rossi.

we're all running short of, something we can't get back — his time. Actually, he gave me his spare time; I was jumping the queue. We were planning to attack the job on a Saturday, but then Adam realised we'd need to do a bit on the Friday night. I couldn't be there, but Adam rolled his sleeves up and went to work anyway. Then, he beat me to work on the Saturday morning. I carefully watched him put together a whole lot of pipe, hook up hydrants, and thoughtfully explain how to make up the sprinklers. He was meticulous. He beavered away as if he was working on his own place.

Eventually I had that awkward conversation about paying someone I knew to do a job for me. He reckoned I couldn't pay him. Even though he was more Elle's friend than mine, even though I didn't really know him that well, he reckoned I couldn't pay him. 'Hey, you do a whole lot for a whole lot of people, and I'm just happy to help a mate out,' he said. This good bastard had given up his Friday night *and* his Saturday to do what he does at least five days a week, and he didn't want anything in return. 'One day,' he said, 'I might need you to help me out. What goes around comes around.'

After Adam had hooked up the big central pipe, a couple of hydrants and two 'strings' of sprinklers, we were able to irrigate 6 hectares, or 20% of our farm. It was a game-changer.

Unfortunately, I wasn't able to return the favour before I needed Adam back. We had drilled in some new grass and it needed watering before it threw the towel in. Twelve months after Adam had hooked up those first 6 hectares, he was back hooking up another six. Another full Saturday of lugging, digging, cutting and connecting in the stinking-hot Central Otago sun that he didn't want paying for. By the end of it, Adam had done half a week's work for nothing. No matter what I said, he wouldn't take any money.

I'd eventually go some way towards paying Adam back. When I had a few lambs killed and processed at the local abattoir, Adam and his partner Nicki got one of them. Later, when we had Hulk killed and processed,

Adam and Nicki got half of him, too. One hundred and fifty-four kilograms of prime beef. These were all animals that had been fattened on feed grown with water that we wouldn't have had in the right place without Adam. He was paying it forward: 'You do something for someone else,' he'd said. I'm regularly asked to do things for other people, and I often think about Adam and what he did for me, and say yes. I don't know if there's a nicer thing you can do for people than give them your time.

THERE ARE PLENTY OF OTHER good bastards in this world. I also reckon there's a higher percentage of them around these parts. You don't have to look far to find them.

One day I was driving in a place on the farm I probably shouldn't have been driving, and I got stuck. Couldn't move forward and couldn't move back, and had to leave my ute stuck where it was and walk home. Within a couple of hours, I had messages from the neighbours either side of us — Robbo on one side, and Paul on the other. 'Do you need a hand to get your ute out?'

If I run into either of those roosters at either end of the day, we'll easily blow off half an hour talking turkey. For the past two seasons Paul and Rachel have let me put my beautiful sheep on their lucerne going into winter. They've never wanted anything for it, but each year they've got a lamb for the freezer. Robbo isn't just my neighbour; he's also my digger driver, source of entertainment, and my relative. Robbo's hilarious. He calls his excavating business Loose Construction, which is highly appropriate. While he's a magician behind the wheel of a digger, or anything else to be fair, he's as loose as you can get — always getting his kit off and playing silly buggers.

One time when I was working in the newsroom, he sent me a wildly inappropriate video. There was Robbo standing in some kind of garage-cum-bar with his pants down to his knees, a stubby in his hand, and his bits hanging out. And while his bits were hanging out, someone about

4 metres away threw a dart at his scrotum. It hit its target and stayed there for what must've been about 30 seconds as blood trickled down Robbo's ball bag and dripped on the floor. The whole thing caught on camera and sent to me in the newsroom. I replied, 'This is classic, Robbo, but what do you want me to do with it?'

He came straight back: 'I dunno — *Seven Sharp*?'

Another time, when Scotty Lee and I were filming a segment for *Country Living* at the Earnscleugh Dog Trials, Robbo ripped his kit off and ran in front of the camera pretending to be a dog punching out a poo before running away again.

Naturally, neither of us is breaking our back to tell people we're related. While Robbo's mum and my dad are first cousins, it's just coincidence that we're neighbours. I'm always buying Robbo a box of beer because he's always doing something for me. Right now, Robbo doesn't have any kids but he's the guy with all the toys. If he's not towing me out of the mud, he's bringing our recycling bin back, or he's feeding out for me, or he's topping my paddock, or shifting my concrete water troughs into place, or dumping a load of gravel on a place that needs a load of gravel dumped, or lending me his spinning-wheel trailer so I can lay out my pipe, or helping me calve a cow, or get my cattle off the busy road.

Robbo's always busy because he's brilliant at what he does, but every time you ask for help he says, 'Yeah, man, we'll make it work.' You'd struggle to find a better neighbour.

Opposite Corey Robinson, aka Robbo.

LAMBING AGAIN — AND CALVING

Above: Feeding out big bales of hay with the aid of only a ute is not recommended. *Photos from Matt's personal collection*

I don't know what I was thinking in 2022, 'cos I was fairly well medicated, but man alive did I spend some money.

I put my $5,000 purebred Swiss Valais Blacknose ram over Dennis's black-face ewes, their 37.5% Valais ewe lambs from the previous season and my two original Valais ewes — those two annoying ones that were yet to produce any girls. About 26 Valais in total. I also put 38 Southdowns to the ram, before sinking into a tough winter. This year, I didn't have any crops planted to feed my sheep or cattle. Whether this was ignorance or disorganisation, I'd later pay for it in both time and money.

The cows were now in calf and approaching two years old, and the ewes were in lamb, and they all needed heaps of tucker I didn't have. So, I bought in a whole lot of hay. Nice wee 'idiot bales' (because only idiots use them) of lucerne for the sheep, and big square bales of lucerne or meadow hay for the cattle. And when all that ran out, I bought more. I must've spent nearly $10,000 on hay that winter — money that would have been earned off farm.

But it got worse. It was easy enough to feed out the little bales of lucerne to the sheep, but feeding out the big bales to the cattle without a tractor was next-level. Those big bales must've weighed about 500 kilograms. I'd park the old flat-deck ute up beside the stack, cut the string on a bale, laboriously break it down like a Weet-Bix and throw slabs of hay on to the ute. Depending on the type of hay, sometimes the slabs would remain relatively intact; other times the back of my ute would resemble a thresh or stook of hay from about 1903. Then I'd drive the old ute out into the middle of the paddock and throw the broken-down bale into the feeder.

After feeding out, I always looked like I'd been sleeping in the hay. On the odd time that the tradies who were chipping away on the last bits of our new house saw me do it, they'd piss themselves laughing. What's worse, I'd often have to do the job at night after I'd done a day's work and all the kids were in bed. Three nights in a row of that malarkey, and you'd have to work pretty bloody hard to see any positives. Still, I only had to do it for about 100 days — then I'd have lambing and my first calving to look forward to.

After feeding out, I always looked like I'd been sleeping in the hay. On the odd time that the tradies who were chipping away on the last bits of our new house saw me do it, they'd piss themselves laughing.

That winter, though, I made a rule for myself: I'd never feed out like that again. I'd either have to buy a tractor or get rid of a heap of cattle.

I had 6 hectares of well-irrigated grass saved up in a paddock above the house, for the last few weeks of winter. I spent thousands of dollars on a new fence cutting that 6 hectares in half so that the cows could be on one half and the ewes the other. Apparently, you want to feed in-lamb ewes and cows much better just before they give birth, and after feeding my animals on bugger-all grass and very expensive hay I wanted to turn a corner in spring, by banging them on all that saved-up grass. Some of my unpaid farm advisers told me it's not common practice to lamb and calve behind a wire, but 'you can do whatever you want'.

I soon learnt why people tend to do what's perhaps more natural and 'spread out' their animals before birthing. As soon as I moved the ewes on to the saved-up grass, some of them started going a bit dopey. They had what's known as sleepy sickness and were walking around like they'd been out on the grog all night. Some of the ewes weren't managing to get enough energy to feed both themselves and their growing lambs. I tried to save them by squirting stuff down their throats and other stuff under their skin, but within a couple of days they'd died. In a cruel twist, though, I was also getting ewes with vaginal prolapses or 'bearings', which some might argue is caused by too much feed prior to lambing. I tried to save them, too, but unsuccessfully. So, while all my sheep were on the same feed I lost half a dozen of them before lambing because I either wasn't feeding them enough or I was feeding them too much.

Then, the lambs started popping out about five days before I thought they were going to, and when I found them they were dead. So much for turning the corner heading into spring. I'd only put 67 ewes to the ram and it took about ten ewes before we got some live lambs on the ground. It was devastating. Did all those animals lose their lives because of me? I love 'fighting' more than anyone I know, and this felt like I'd been training my guts out all year for a big fight and had been knocked out in the first round.

I got Southdown breeder Dave Robertson, who's also a vet, on the blower and asked him why my lambs weren't surviving. 'It could be abortion caused by salmonella or toxoplasmosis or campylobacter,' he said. 'I'm in your area tomorrow, so I'll come for a look.' It didn't take long for Dave to see where I could be going wrong. There were lots of possibilities. Maybe I shouldn't be lambing behind an electric fence, maybe I should've chosen a more sheltered paddock, maybe I shouldn't have shorn my sheep before lambing, maybe I shouldn't be carrying so many older ewes and, by the look of the small dead lambs, maybe I could've fed those ewes a little better over winter and leading up to lambing. Dave took away some dead

lambs that day, had them tested, and ruled out the abortion possibility, which was at least something.

About a year later, I figured out that I'd somehow miscalculated my lambing date. I should've had them on that grass, that better feed, about a week before I did. How could I — a supposedly smart-enough bloke — stuff up something so simple? One of the biggest problems with this game is that if you make mistakes, they can be fatal and that can really hurt. Anyway, I pretty much took down those electric fences with one hand that day as I waved goodbye to Dave with the other.

Things weren't a whole lot better in the cow paddock. The first calf of the season, the first calf born on our property, surprised me by also coming early. I found it dead in a very small creek and I found that heart-breaking. I reckon calves are one of the most beautiful creatures in the world. On top of that, its mother almost killed me as I carried its lifeless carcass out of the paddock. Never get between a cow and its new-born calf — even if the calf is dead. On the land I'm always learning, and I'm almost always learning lessons the hard way.

Thankfully, the lambs started surviving just as people had said they would and I began crunching the numbers. Even though comparison can be a bit of a killer, I was forever trying to work out how we were tracking. How did we compare against other farmers? They always told me they were getting around a 150% lambing mark, even though the internet told me the national average was just 128. After our really rough start we were now looking like being better than average — but then some of the triplet lambs started dying, and we also had issues closer to home. The pet lambs — the ones we were bottle-feeding at least three times a day for weeks, the ones the kids had named and we'd got attached to — started getting crook and dying. We think they got bloat, which other people seem to reckon is caused by a build-up of bacteria in the stomach, which can stem from overfeeding.

Once they're sick, lambs can die within hours. Thinking that one of the lambs was on its last legs, I made the ten-minute trip into Alex with it sitting on my lap. Without a word of a lie, it took its last breath as I carried it across the car park at the vet clinic. The drive home was fairly shit.

We ended up getting just 38 lambs from 38 Southdown ewes that season, so 100%. Another Southdown breeder in the valley later told me 'You're doing well to get 100% from Southdowns here', but 100% wasn't good enough for me. It's below average and I don't want to be below average. I started falling into a bit of a hole.

> **We had some visitors in the September school holidays, who reminded me just how lucky we are to be living where we are and doing what we're doing. Their enthusiasm was infectious.**

Meanwhile, the hybrid vigour of the Valais ram over the black-face sheep helped them lamb at 125%. The two original Valais had triplets. AND — they finally produced some girls. Three of them. I wasn't cursed after all. After that frustratingly slow start, I was finally out of the breeding-up blocks. However, after a tough winter, some bad news on the work front and what felt like a reasonably poor lambing, I continued to struggle for a bit.

Then we had some visitors in the September school holidays, who reminded me just how lucky we are to be living where we are and doing what we're doing. Their enthusiasm was infectious. Elle's great friend Joy and her three kids, Jono, Stella and Annabelle, were down from Christchurch, while my best mate Tuffers and his two kids, Max and Eva, came across from Queenstown. They were the first people to stay with us at 'The Land'. The kids fed pet lambs, rode on the back of the ute, biked around the farm to check on whether any cows were calving, and asked 15 million, 336 thousand mostly delightful questions.

Late in the day, we noticed that one of the beasts we bucket-fed was showing signs of calving. We all hoped that the kids, who weren't from the country, would see their first calf being born, but its mum wouldn't play ball. I'd pulled out my phone and punched in something like: 'How long do you have to calve a cow?' The information immediately bounced back: 'The calf should be delivered within 2 to 5 hours of the appearance of the water bag.' I'm the kind of guy who could wait weeks if necessary to make sure an animal arrives safely, and at some point I realised that if the calf wasn't born by about one or two o'clock in the morning I'd have to roll up my sleeves and get involved.

Hours after everyone else had gone to bed, that was exactly how it played out. The beautiful black cow with the white face laboured away for hours without any luck. I needed to help, but couldn't catch her. Without any yards to put her in, and with that deadline looming, I thought that if I ran her in to a gap between a fence-line and an open gate, I could try to pull the calf out. I ran her in to the gap, but she quickly jumped out of it and on to the drive — which leads to State Highway 85. Time for a quick Plan B. If I got her close to what can be quite a busy road, I could open a gate and run her in to the triangle paddock, which had a small shelter that AP and I had built for the sheep the first year we were here. That sheep shelter was as close as I could get to a set of cattle yards at this point.

The plan was risky, but it was now after midnight and I was short on time. So I got in front of the cow, opened the gate to the triangle paddock and cut her off at the pass. It was almost like she knew the plan and wanted to be part of it. Once she was in the paddock, I ran her in to the shelter. That went as smoothly as the step before, but then it got interesting again. Under the lights of my ute, I put my hand inside the cow, hoping to find two front feet and a head. Instead, I pulled out a tail. The cow had been struggling away for hours because she was giving birth backwards. Bugger! I wondered what the hell I was supposed to do now. I don't like asking for help, especially when it's about half past twelve in the morning. Back to Google. 'What are the chances of a calf surviving after being born backwards?' The answer: 'Only a few backward calves are small enough to be pulled by hand . . . Most calves don't survive a backward birth unless you get them out quickly.'

Top: The cow who gave birth backwards posing with her wee new-born. **Above**: Our friends' kids riding on the back of my ute with Bede and Finn that same day. *Photos from Matt's personal collection*

Shit. I wonder how long I've got to get the wee bugger out? Or is it a big bugger? There's no time for thought, I've got to pull my finger out and get to work. And I pull like I've never pulled before, but the calf doesn't come. I'm by myself, but I'm talking and I'm yelling and the language is terrible. Then I wedge myself between the cow and the fence behind me. My feet are pushing hard up against the fence and I'm pulling and at times I can't even remember what I was pulling, but after about half an hour — seems like half a week — a little black calf comes sliding out of that cow. 'Most calves don't survive a backward birth' is at the front of my mind, and that little black beauty doesn't move for what seems like the other half of that week. I want it to move more than anything I've wanted before. I lightly slap its face, clear the goo from its mouth, and then — after what was realistically about 20 seconds — the wee calf shakes its head. It's alive. I am ecstatic.

I've lambed a few ewes before, but calving your first cow, and backwards at that — a cow that you bucket-fed when it was a calf itself — at half past one in the morning, is one of the greatest feelings I've ever had. Still, both the cow and I were exhausted. My arms felt like lead. I also had to demolish half the shelter to get the new mum out of it and on to her calf. I stayed there for an hour, watching the cow clean up her calf, before making my weary way home to bed.

This game will break your heart, and melt it, all in the same day.

IT'S TAKEN ME A WHILE to figure this out, but for a self-described 'very average bloke' I'm a reasonably high achiever. I always want to do a really good job of everything I do and that, at times, can cause problems. For example, I'm usually really time-poor because it usually takes me so bloody long to do anything. When I was starting out on 'The Land', a smart man suggested that the best thing for a busy bloke like me to do on a small place like ours was just buy in 'one-year ewes' — sheep that have one more productive year of their life left — lamb them in spring and then sell all the ewes and lambs in summer. That way I wouldn't have to winter anything. Winter can be real hard yakka down on the farm. I guess one day, maybe, I'll do that, but for now I want to have a red-hot go at breeding really good stock, the kind of stock that other people want to buy and breed from. My philosophy has always been: 'If you don't have a go, you'll never know.' Also, I'm not farming for money; I'm doing it as a hobby, for the love of it, because if I'm only going to live once I want to spend some of that life farming, even if it is on a really small scale.

I've always found, though, that one of the biggest problems in life is that you don't know what you don't know. More specifically, as a part-time farmer you don't know what it's like to breed sheep and cattle on 72 acres until you're actually breeding sheep and cattle on 72 acres. There were another couple of things I was yet to figure out: first, could I actually produce decent animals; and second, even if I *could* produce decent animals, would real farmers actually take me seriously, and buy them?

I've always found, though, that one of the biggest problems in life is that you don't know what you don't know.

Farmers who breed sheep and cattle for other people to breed from have to cull (meaning get rid of) any animals that aren't good enough to breed from. If, typically, the same number of ewe and ram lambs are born every year and one ram can go on to service more than a hundred ewes, then most rams aren't needed for the reproductive process, right? While we're here asking questions, how good would it be to be a ram that makes the grade?

In my first two years of breeding Southdown rams I was lucky enough to sell all my ram lambs, four in my first year and six in my second year. Now, with 350% more Southdown sheep in my third year of breeding, that would change.

With all the problems we had, we'd managed to produce just 38

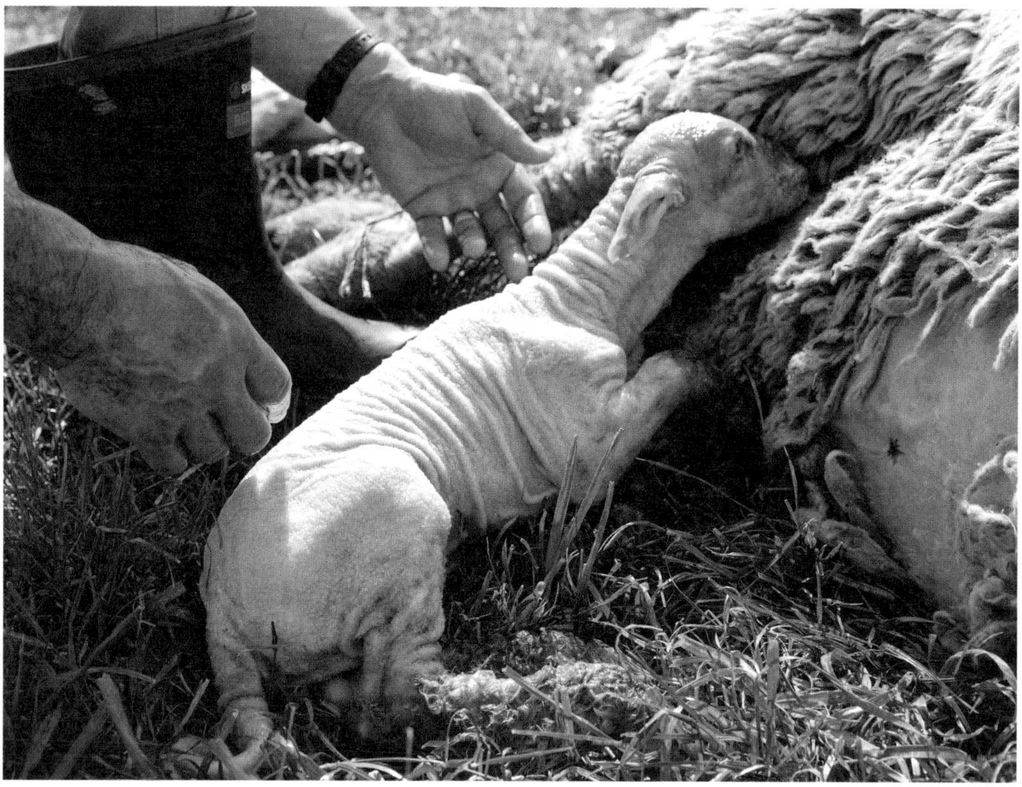

Southdown lambs from 38 Southdown ewes. At six months of age, apparently it was time for some culling, and Rob Hall, a Southdown ram breeder mate of mine, wanted to help out. I also think he wanted to have a better look at 'The Land 202/22', my good ram lamb sired by JJ that cleaned up at the Invercargill A&P Show (more on this later). I think he wanted to see if he could get a good deal on the ram before any other bugger noticed.

First, Rob and I culled three of the nineteen ewe lambs, leaving me with a very tidy sixteen including '268', the lamb with the broken leg costing hundreds of dollars in vet bills and milk powder, who was destined for the 'house paddock'. Then we cut the ram lambs in half. Within minutes we'd split nineteen ram lambs into two mobs. A mob of keepers, and a mob of killers . . . and if you're an animal you don't want to end up in the 'killers' mob. The keepers were the superior rams I'd try to sell to farmers, while the killers were destined for the freezer. Not mine; perhaps it's snobbish, but I don't want to eat a ram.

Immediately after sorting the ram lambs into these two lines, I felt a little sick. After watching my beautiful big boys grow for half a year, I really didn't like the idea of cutting the heads off half of them, even though I knew it was probably the right thing to do from a business sense — as a stud breeder, you really should only sell your best animals. Still, '237' and '238' — the lambs the kids called 'John' and 'John 2' — were in the killers mob and that, especially, was a little hard to swallow. I'd bottle-fed those wee buggers hundreds of times and I wanted them to have a longer life as opposed to a shorter one. If they weren't good enough to be used as stud sires, maybe I could sell them to lifestylers, kids, a bloody zoo — anyone. This is the kind of thing I think a lot about nowadays — rather than obsessing over current affairs or politics — and I don't even know if I'm ashamed of that.

The fateful day was still in the future so it actually didn't matter whether they were in the keepers or the killers mob; all of them would

Opposite Me and Scotty lambing a ewe.

live for at least another three or four months. And as for 237 and 238, who were just a little too tall and lean for Rob and me, they would eventually become two of the luckiest lambs this side of the Waitaki River.

Again, we started running out of feed towards the end of winter. I put my older in-lamb ewes and Southdown ewe hoggets behind a wire on ryecorn. Tastes like shit, apparently, but in the absence of anything else, they'll eat it. I had two other small mobs to deal with, though — eighteen rams and ram lambs in one mob and nine in-lamb Swiss Valais Blacknose ewe hoggets in another, and because the grass had stopped growing in the cold weather I was feeding them some of those terribly expensive small bales of lucerne hay, which is like crack cocaine for sheep. Yep — those 'idiot bales'. I can't get enough of them, which probably tells you quite a bit about me.

Anyway, it came time to actually get rid of the unwanted ram lambs, which wasn't going to be good for 237 and 238. A few other breeders had told me the best thing to do with cull ram lambs was send them to the freezing works, because if you took them to a sale there'd always be 'some tight old bugger who sees them going cheap and decides to buy them and use them over their ewes'. The problem was, I only had seven cull ram lambs to get rid of: five Southdowns and a couple of Valais crosses, and that many wasn't worth troubling a drafter from one of the meat companies. But there was another option. As a kid growing up in Milton, I'd often headed through to the Clutha sale with Dad. I have great memories of checking out all the yarded sheep and cattle, watching my dad auction, and 'bidding' on stock that were destined for someone else. This is what I'd do.

As soon as I had a spare Wednesday in my diary I was off to the Clutha sale — at least 35 years since I'd last been. The big draft happened the afternoon before and the seven culls camped in a borrowed trailer overnight. My trip down Memory Lane started early: it's a two-hour drive from Chatto Creek to Balclutha and the sheep needed to be yarded by 8.45 a.m. It felt like I was there in no time. I was so excited. A stock sale is right up there with an A& P Show as one of my favourite things. Animals and people. Heaps of both. Perfect.

My biggest fear was having to back the trailer in front of real men, but on this day I *nailed* it. James, a friendly young agent who I'd met before, helped me load the lambs off the trailer. 'Are these two-tooths?' he asked, thinking that the sheep were older than they were — a good sign. I exchanged small-talk with a few agents and farmers as I checked out the sheep and cattle on offer. People seem to like that I'm having a go, albeit a really small one. I then took in the start of the cattle sale, which probably hadn't changed in four decades, before heading back to the sheep.

My biggest fear was having to back the trailer in front of real men, but on this day I *nailed* it.

My ram lambs were up first, but there weren't many people there. Not like I remembered back in the day. It was worrying. With lamb prices being low at the time I thought I was going to get a hiding, but my five Southdowns sold quickly for $162 each; the two Valais for 160. All bought by someone from the same outfit running the sale — Rural Livestock. The agent was apparently buying them on behalf of a meat company. As I'd thought, my seven cull ram lambs, including 237 and 238, would have a relatively short life and end up on someone's plate.

Maybe less than an hour after it started, the sheep section of the Clutha sale was done; but the trading wasn't over. An old fella I'd met previously at a shearing fund-raiser had been busy watching the cattle auction and had missed the entire sheep section of the sale. He was checking out my Southdown ram lambs as I walked past and I heard him mention how good they were. He especially appreciated their long length, saying, 'They'd go really well over my Romney ewes.' I told the guy that the lambs used to be mine but they'd been bought by a meat company. Then, the agent who'd bought them on behalf of that meat company piped up: 'You can buy them if you want.'

I wasn't sure who he'd be buying them off — I figured I'd already sold 'em. But my old mate would eventually hand-pick the bottle-fed brothers 237 and 238 out of the pen, paying me 200 bucks each for them and potentially prolonging their deaths for years. Unbelievable. After hours and hours of agonising over the fate of these creatures, they were saved, at the last minute, from Death Row. Old mate's cobber bought another of the cull Southdown rams for the same price. That day I took seven lambs to the sale and sold four of them once and three of them twice. I drove home with a smile wrapped right across my face for the whole of the two hours.

I NOW HAD SEVEN GOOD ram lambs to sell, and the plan was to do that in ram-selling season, sometime in December. One Saturday afternoon, while tapping away at another chapter of this book, I got a text from Blair Robertson from Merrydowns. He's that bloke with the biggest Southdown stud in the world — the bloke I bought most of my Southdown sheep from.

'Where are the pigs? [Nickname for Southdowns.] We've just gone past. Just going to see Sally's brother's house. If you're about, we'll call in for five minutes on our way home.' Blair wanted to have a look at those seven good ram lambs ahead of me selling them in about four months' time. Now, to me Blair Robertson is a sheep-breeding god. His thoughts on my prized young pigs, positioned pride of place in the paddock in front of the house, could either make me or break me. Scary.

Blair jumps out of the car in his usual enthusiastic way, but there's no time for even a quick drink. In early August, we're losing the light quickly. We scale the fence and beeline it for the rams. 'Shit, they're looking good,' says Blair. I make a gag about the two Valais rams in amongst the Southdowns, but Blair only has eyes for the one breed. 'You could have two or three stud sires there,' he says. I'm tickled pink. As hard as it is being an inexperienced bloke breeding sheep on a small bit of dirt without decent infrastructure, Blair's words are enough to keep me going for another couple of years. About an hour after he leaves, I get another text from him. 'Cheers for showing us your sheep mate. They look real good. Maybe we could do a swap with a sire instead of buying one.'

The biggest, and arguably the best, Southdown breeder in the *world* wanted to use one of my rams for his stud. I couldn't possibly get a better endorsement for my sheep and I was also incredibly excited about a Merrydowns ram turning up at 'The Land' sometime soon.

In fairy-tale fashion, though, it got even better. I woke up in Greymouth one morning in late October to a text from Blair. 'Hey mate. Where are you selling your rams?' I replied as I usually do, using ten times as many words as the person I'm communicating with — even though I only have seven rams to sell, it's complicated. Blair comes back to me: 'Do you want to put the top ones up at our ram sale?'

Blair's ram sale could be the biggest Southdown ram sale in the world. Near-nude and alone, I immediately start performing somersaults on the four-poster bed. I eventually come to and text back, revealing all my insecurities. 'Oooohhhh shit mate I'd love to . . . But after you pick one out for you, do you think they'd be good enough?'

And Blair, a bloke who's known for being as blunt as a hammer, goes: 'Honestly mate, they are good enough.'

Two days later, Blair's on his way to 'The Land'. I've yarded the rams, and when he sees them for the first time in months, he starts laughing. I instantly think there's something wrong with them. Grinning widely under his iconic orange towelling hat, he says, 'Shit, Matt — what have you been feeding them? They're *huge* . . . they must be 120, 130 kilograms.'

Running his hands over them, Blair checks their feet and their mouths. 'They're no bloody good if they can't walk and they can't eat,' he says. He lets them into a bigger pen, lets them run around and watches the way they move, the way they carry themselves.

'That one's a paddler, it's no good. Cull the one that's a bit shitty — it's a presentation thing, you know all about that.'

Three out of seven made the grade, with a fourth being culled after

Blair checked his balls. We talked sheep for about an hour before he loaded up the best three to take them home. 'I need to strip a bit of fat off 'em, Matt, harden them up a bit.' I couldn't have been any happier. Two years earlier I'd trekked down to Blair and Sally's Merrydowns ram sale in Waikoikoi, West Otago. They sell a couple of hundred Romney and Southdown rams every year to farmers and breeders from all over the country. The day runs as slick as *1News*, and for me, nowadays at least, is a whole lot cooler. It didn't seem to matter that I'd simply bought some good ewes and a good ram, put them together and kept some of the lambs alive. Now, it felt like I had just confirmed that three of my sons had made the All Blacks, and I was chuffed. Writing this, I'm just ten days away from going to Blair's sale and I'm pretty pumped. Others understand the excitement. Just yesterday I talked about it on Jamie McKay's *The Country* radio show. Farming is tough going. Breeding sheep is tough going. But moments like that make it all worth it.

THERE WAS PLENTY MORE TO learn. Having wintered nineteen in-calf cows, plus a few extras, on some really expensive hay, nineteen calves were born in spring. It was a special time. The whole family would stop whatever we were doing to watch a cow birthing, although often the calves would take their sweet time and I'd be the only one patient enough to see the whole process through to the end. One of the cows had twin heifer calves, which apparently only occurs in about 2% of beef cattle pregnancies, but it meant we still managed to land nineteen calves from nineteen cows despite losing that very first wee calf. Interestingly, one of my white Speckle Parks hadn't got in calf; she was more than likely a twin and what's known as a freemartin — born with a male as the other twin, and sterile.

My two Highland cows hadn't got in calf either, probably because they weren't mature enough. Wanting them to both pay their way and have some cute calves on the place, I left Hamish running with them for months to see what would happen. Eventually it paid dividends. Well, kind of. Five months after all the other cows had calved, Creamy Milk had 'Waitangi', a caramel-coloured heifer calf, on Waitangi weekend, and four months after that Robbo and I pulled a bull calf, 'King', out of Gingernut on King's Birthday weekend in June. Yep — the start of winter. It's a lucky thing that Highlands are born with two coats of hair.

In the meantime, with all those new calves on the ground there were a lot of mouths to feed. This was fine in spring with all the grass that had grown, but not so flash when the summer drought hit. The plan was to keep my cows and calves on until weaning in March, when I could sell them all and pay some big tax bills I'd run up after spending our tax money on building the new house. I was doing my best to irrigate some of the ryecorn; it was planted on our 'second block', which hadn't been set up for irrigation yet. This was a temporary fix, but I never really had much feed stored up ahead of the cattle eating it. At one point I reckon I had about a week of tucker left before I was in the crap. Someone suggested that I sell my cows and calves immediately — what they call 'all counted' or 'cows with calves at foot'. It wasn't part of the plan, but it was damn tempting. I wouldn't have to spend so much time irrigating, and if I didn't have as many cattle I wouldn't have to worry about what I was going to feed them.

But I always knew that if I was going to quit my cattle early, I'd pay for it. I rang an agent, who reckoned the nineteen cows and their calves, so 38 animals, would only be worth about 700 bucks each at that time. That was just over 25 grand. But if I could hold on to them for another five or six weeks, the cows would be worth about $1,500 and the calves about 650 — meaning 40 grand. I would lose about $15,000 by selling my cows and calves earlier than planned, and I couldn't afford to lose that kind of money with the tax bills looming. I thought about buying in some feed to keep my cattle going, but every time we spent money on the farm it came out of off-farm income and that was starting to hurt.

I was running out of ideas and I was worrying myself sick. Then, I ran

into my new mate, OB, outside Ōmakau's Muddy Creek cafe. I'd first met John 'OB' O'Brien eighteen months earlier, following an after-dinner talk I did in Palmerston North. The youngest of twelve children, OB is a former stock agent who farms in both the Manawatū and Central Otago. He's a real mover and shaker. This former footy player is an affable older rooster with some of the best one-liners you'll ever hear. I ran into him again the next day at the iconic Fielding Saleyards, one of the largest in the Southern Hemisphere. With his warm nature and brilliant banter he seemed to know, talk and laugh with everyone, including me, and I really liked the cut of his jib. Shit, he must've cut some deals in those saleyards. OB's well connected. OB's smooth. The kind of guy who remembers your kids' names and always asks after them. Right off the bat, I think we both knew we'd become cobbers.

Anyway, eighteen months later, here we are chatting outside Ōmakau's cafe.

'How you getting on, boy?' he says.

'Not great, OB — you?'

He replies, 'Fit as a fiddle. What's the problem?'

I tell him about being overstocked in the dry, about what I'd get for my cattle if I sold them now, and about not being sure what to do next.

OB reckoned that 'all counted' price was about right, but he had other ideas. After confirming just how many cows and calves I had, he said: 'I'll take 'em — I'll find a place for twenty cows and calves, no worries.' I thanked him, but told him it didn't really feel right for me to send my problem to someone else, considering that they were facing the same problem. 'Fair enough,' he said. 'Leave it with me.'

A few days later the phone rings, and it's OB. 'Are you home, boy? I'm on the road — I'll be there in about half an hour.'

Exactly half an hour later, while I'm sitting at the table tapping away on the computer, I see a big green tractor coming over the brow of the hill. There's a trailer behind the tractor, and on top of that trailer there looks to be about ten or twelve big round bales of baleage. Baleage is like gold in a drought. That load is probably worth about $1,500. And it's baleage I probably can't afford. Not sure what's going to happen here.

If you want to know what a hero looks like, well, sometimes it looks like OB driving towards you in the middle of a drought in a big green tractor towing a big old trailer full of baleage. The boys and I run out and open the gates. There's a few hellos and a quick chat about where to put the bales, and then OB ditches the trailer, picks up the boys, and we start unloading. My wee fellas are in the cab with OB — I'm watching from the ground — and all three Chisholm boys are smiling from ear to ear.

'These cattle are like kids with a box of chocolates,' OB says. 'They'll eat all this tucker in one day if you let 'em.' Using electric fence standards and a hot wire, he shows me how to slowly feed those bales to the cattle. 'This should get you through to weaning.'

I was out of jail, but what would it cost me?

'Nothing. I just had 'em spare lying around. They're worth next to nothing to me, and a whole lot to you — so you can have 'em.'

As predicted, at weaning I sold sixteen Speckle Park cows on Trade Me for $1,550 each. They were that popular I could have sold 'em three times over. I sold their steer calves to our neighbour Pete for $700 each, and the heifer calves went to a fella in Canterbury for 600. All the money went to the Inland Revenue Department.

I'm not sure how to pay OB back, but I want to, and one day, one day, somehow, I will.

Above: OB and his big green tractor coming to our rescue.
Photos from Matt's personal collection

SKELLERUP
RED BAND

DOWN AND UP AGAIN

A few years ago, when I was working as a TV reporter and host, I learnt that I was dealing with grief, burnout and depression. Now I might've left the newsroom but, for an anxious person, going freelancing and farming really meant I was jumping out of the fat and into the fire. Coming out of the 2022/2023 drought, I couldn't shake off my negativity; my negative thoughts began to consume me. They robbed me of all my joy, and I really started struggling.

One of the reasons why I started struggling all over again, was because I was supposed to be some kind of mental health advocate now, but I was losing it myself. Another thing that really got me was doing a budget, which I did while I had Covid. As a freelancer with no set income, I was wondering how I was going to pay the mortgage — how was I going to make that kind of money each month? Given the cost-of-living crisis we were going through, I thought I was going to lose everything. My anxiety was next-level. I was overestimating the size of the problem and underestimating my ability to solve it — which is anxiety in a nutshell.

I eventually realised that I was always worried about *something*. Spending my tax money on building a new house during the pandemic. Selling those cows and their calves to cover my tax bills. During the drought, I worried about whether I could feed my cows in a week's time; after that, I worried about whether those cows were in calf, because if they *were* in calf they were worth about $500 more apiece. And once OB had saved my bacon with the baleage, I worried about whether I could sell them. When I did sell them and paid my tax, I immediately started worrying about how I was going to pay my tax the following year.

It was the kind of worry that robbed me of all joy. I couldn't think about anything else. I was miserable at the dinner table. I was miserable taking my medicine — farming. Then, my old psychologist from Auckland sent me a message. He must've picked up on the fact that I was battling — those guys are telepathic. Just fifteen minutes into a much-needed session, he said: 'Matt, you've got GAD — Generalised Anxiety Disorder.' This basically means I could represent New Zealand in worrying, which is quite cool because I've never represented New Zealand in anything.

For me, the Mental Health Foundation's 'Five Ways to Wellbeing' are key. I need to connect, be active, take notice, keep learning and give back.

It was a diagnosis that explained almost everything; a diagnosis that explained my entire life — initially running away from the tough stuff with the help of booze and drugs, then tackling the tough stuff but working so hard at suppressing my anxiety that I became burnt out and depressed.

Having a diagnosis helps; it means I know what I'm dealing with. I know I have to find ways to get rid of the GAD, and now I want to do that entirely naturally. I've had a couple more sessions with Jock — we're looking into whether I'm also dealing with impulsivity and ADHD, which, one could argue, fuels my anxiety. To curb all this, I can't get too complacent. I need to constantly remind myself to look after myself. I need to do things that get me 'out of my head'.

For me, the Mental Health Foundation's 'Five Ways to Wellbeing' are key. I need to connect, be active, take notice, keep learning and give back.

One of the best things I've done for my overactive, anxious mind, though, is get plenty of sleep. Often I'll get the kids in bed and then immediately jump into bed myself. Sleep is the best drug, and when I get enough of that drug everything seems so much better. My worries often just fade away; I find it so much easier to turn negatives into positives, and to find joy in every day. And despite the pressures of farming and earning a living, when you're on the land and in a small community, there's joy everywhere. Nowadays, I live for 'glimmers' — small moments that spark joy or peace.

ONE OF THE REASONS WE moved to the country was that we were craving community, craving real connection. We have it in spades now. Most of the time we're at Chatto Creek we're living the dream, and the Lees, who are just over the road, are a big part of that. In the summer of 2022/2023 we spent a lot of time together, swimming in the river or at Falls Dam. The kids used a big rope to fling themselves off the bank into the Manuherikia. They kayaked and swam. Scotty cooked sausages on his wee barbie. I talked a lot. We all enjoyed unplugging for a bit.

A couple of times now, we've given the Lees some of our lamb we've had killed and processed. A couple of times now, Scotty's cooked some of our lamb, invited us all to theirs and we've all enjoyed a great meal together. These are amazing nights. They're fun. And they're wholesome. It feels like we're really living. We've spent the last three New Years at their place and had a bloody ball, and this year we're all heading away camping together. I can't wait. We're so lucky to have the Lees living just over the road — they make our life here so much better.

Another of the things I've loved about going country is watching the rest of the family flourish. Elle, like me, has probably never been busier, but often says: 'I love my life.' As well as being a brilliant mother to our three kids, Bede (now seven), Finn (five) and Bree (two), she also works full-time as an Itinerary Delivery Manager for Ahipara Luxury Travel, a company that deals with high-end holidaymakers from all over the world.

Elle's the most diligent employee I know. When we're both working from home, she actually doesn't talk to me — she reckons she's so busy that she doesn't have time to answer my questions. It's quite annoying, actually, because I need a bit of hand-holding.

Elle's very social, has a lot of friends, and enjoys spending time with her family. She's always visiting her parents, Dennis and Christine, and her sister Bridget. She's also found her 'thing' — she's rediscovered running and beats her feet for hours every week. In August 2023 she went to Australia's Northern Territory to run an 85-kilometre staged ultra-marathon, and won her 25- to 39-year-old women's category. Next was the Queenstown marathon. She trains hard. Driving home from the kids' football in Cromwell or Queenstown or Wānaka, we'll drop Elle off in Clyde so she can run the final 19 kilometres home. She says running is meditation for people who can't sit still. It's her time out; time when she's able to clear her head and reset. It's always a bit of a juggling act, though. I'll be out on the farm mucking about with the stock, and I'll receive a text: 'I'd really like to run for 90 minutes this afternoon and I don't want to run in the dark. The dinner's made, you just have to heat it up. How much longer are you going to be?'

Elle can handle a lot, but I'm very aware of how much pressure she's under when I'm away for work — and I'm away often. There's our three rambunctious children, their education and their sports. All the animals need to be fed and watered, and in spring the pet lambs need to be given milk up to five times a day. Elle just rolls her sleeves up and rips into it while I pester her with messages from all over the country. 'How are you getting on? How are the kids? Any new lambs?' Her — often short — replies are always an indication of how little time she has available. 'No lambs. Kids fine. When are you home?' I hope she doesn't have to put up with me being away so often for much longer.

The kids are thriving. Bede and Finn are different boys from when we lived in Auckland, and both seem to be excelling at the local Omakau School. Bede has even been described as a 'rock-star student'. His reports

have been so glowing that I've actually wondered whether he's really my son. He's smart, curious and kind. We're told that wee Finn, who likes to push the boundaries a little more at home, is a model student at school. Finn's tough, and doesn't take any shit. They're loving their sport, too. Whatever they're playing, they're both really competitive; they want to be on the ball, they want to be where the action is. Just like their old man did.

On a weekend in spring, our whole family will spend hours watching calves and lambs being born. Whatever's happening down on the farm, the kids ask heaps of questions, trying to understand their world.

On the farm, Bede, especially, is becoming really handy. At lambing time I'm forever trying to catch a sheep to treat its feet, or give it a shot of penicillin, or lamb it. Once I've caught the damn sheep, Bede will bring over the gear to get the job done, then hold the sheep down until I've finished doing the job. Sometimes the job takes longer because of the kids' 'help' but, of course, most of the time that doesn't matter.

On a weekend in spring, our whole family will spend hours watching calves and lambs being born. Whatever's happening down on the farm, the kids ask heaps of questions, trying to understand their world. When they can't help, they find other things to do. They whack down thistles: 'Let's get the buggers!' They swim in water troughs, sometimes nude. They throw stones into ponds. They make those birthday cakes out of cow shit. And sometimes, when they're in the ute and they're noisy or they're fighting or they're whingeing, they annoy the crap out of me — but those days just make you more appreciative of the good ones.

The boys really started coming into their own when we moved on to the land. One day, without us realising, they packed a couple of bags with a whole heap of clothes, food and water.

'Where are you going, boys?'

Above: Bede (left) and Finn heading off on their big adventure.
Photos from Matt's personal collection

'We're going on an adventure.'

'That sounds exciting. When are you coming back home?'

'Sometime tomorrow.'

An hour later, they're home; hungry, thirsty and exhausted, but happy.

It took me fifteen months to throw some grass seed around our new house to create a lawn, and although that might sound lazy, it was one of the best things we ever didn't do. When the boys added water to the dirt that surrounded their new home, they had the time of their lives. We must've carried the kids, covered from head to toe in mud, into one of the showers at least ten times. Probably about another ten times, they would've made their own way into the shower, leaving a trail of mud all through the house.

Bree loves the farming, too. For a long time I didn't think I'd have kids, and when we started having kids I didn't think we'd have a girl, and when we had a girl it was better than great. Bree and I have a special relationship. Every time I say, 'Who wants to come farming?', Bree's always quick to throw up her hand and yell, 'Meeeeeee!' She could spend an hour in her car seat watching Dad beavering away out the window. Every time I head back to check in, she's happy as.

Sometimes we actually get off the farm. Sometimes, not often, we head through to Queenstown so the kids can play at the jump parks or video game places. Generally, though, I don't want to go far. I love it here. Sure, it gets really hot. And really cold. Sure, sometimes the wind blows so fiercely that the only place you can safely be is inside. But I genuinely believe we live in paradise. We're so lucky to be able to live here. We're so lucky to be able to live on some land and experience the elements. Experience nature. We're so lucky to be able to learn about animals and their lifecycles. About plants and what makes them grow. We're so lucky to be able to better understand how it's all connected. This is such a good place to live. To just be. Whether we're in the Ōmakau, Ophir or Alexandra pool, or in the Manuherikia River, we've always got our togs on and we're in the water. We visit the country pubs for a feed, a drink, and a chat with the locals. We ride bikes on the rail trail, pick apples off trees at the side of the road, and pull 'yabbies' out of dams.

One freezing-cold winter's day we decided to get out of the house and drive up to the Poolburn Dam. It's a different world up there. An oasis. Black sharp-edged rocks jut out of the dry ground. Rustic huts look out over it all. On this day, the cold wind cuts the kids in half and whips water off the dam up into the air. It doesn't put the boys off. 'Dad, let's go yabbying!' A line with a small piece of meat on a hook goes into the drink. We all peer into the crystal-clear water and watch the lobsters leave their homes to investigate. Claws out. They take the bait. One or two at a time. The kids are as excited as they have ever been. 'We've got another one — no we've got two . . . This is amazing, oh my god this is more fun than Queenstown.'

The best things in life are free, and the best things are all around us.

'C'mon, boys — we've got enough for a wee feed. It's bloody freezing. Let's jump in the ute and go home.'

'No, Dad, this is the best day ever — just a few more. Please, Dad!'

THE ŌMAKAU RACES, IN EARLY January, are almost bigger than Christmas around these parts. Almost hotter than the sun. One year, Bede said, excitedly, 'Dad, Mum gave me two bucks and I put it on Hurricane Hill.'

'Why did you put it on Hurricane Hill, mate?' I asked.

'Because I liked the name.'

'Bede, I like the name, too — but if that horse comes in first, and it won't, I'll give you a hundred bucks.'

Hurricane Hill, of course, came in first and I had to hand over 100 slides to my oldest child. A few days later, a whole lot of carny folk came to town with some life-size dinosaurs and that hundred bucks was burning a hole in Bede's pocket. He'd go on to learn a valuable lesson that day: once he spent some money, he'd no longer have it.

Bede bought two stuffed toys off the carnies, one for him and one for

his best friend, Louis — which was admirable, but when he got home he was gutted that he no longer had his hundred bucks. Louis's mum, Suzy, paid Bede back and I gave him a few bucks I owed him for helping on the farm. Now Bede had his hundred dollars again.

That night, when I was lying beside him trying to get him to sleep, I told him of another way he could spend his hundred dollars. 'Little buddy, if you buy two Swiss Blacknose sheep off me, and those sheep have ewe lambs, you might be able to turn your $100 into $1,000.'

Bede was sold, but — just like his old man at first — Bede's ewes had boys. Still, he now knows the difference between buying something for fun and buying something as an investment, and he's bound to get some girls in the next few years. I reckon country kids can have a great education away from school as well as at school.

IT'S ALSO REALLY NICE TO be able to help out the community we live in.

One year I spoke at the Central Otago Winter Feed Competition. Two years later, I emcee'd the night. I'm pretty sure we raised nearly $100,000 for our two local primary schools and the Otago Southland Rescue Helicopter Trust that night. A whole lot of people do a whole lot of work to put these nights together, and I just roll in at the last minute and try to make people laugh. I'm going to go out on a limb and estimate that about 1,000 people live across the Manuherikia and Ida valleys. And about 200 of them cram into Alexandra's RSA for those winter feed nights.

We might be celebrating crop yields and dry matter figures, but those nights are far from dry. They'd have to be some of the best nights of my life. Almost all of the adults in our community coming together to have a good time, and when I'm emcee-ing I make sure we laugh at each other and at ourselves. They tell me that back in the day there used to be cracking community parties in wee country halls about every three weeks, right across the nation. In a way, these winter crop nights are like going back 50 years, but weirdly, I reckon they're the future.

Another night, I hosted 'Matakanui's Got Talent' in the Becks Memorial Hall. A bloke from Queenstown pulled rabbits out of a hat, Paul Doughery's band belted out some '80s classics, and local legend OB, my good mate, was a terrible, yet very entertaining, Elvis. We raised about $35,000 for the school. I drove home sober but high as a kite, thinking how lucky we are living in such a neat little community and how bloody nice it is to play a small part in it.

I spend quite a bit of time and money at the PGG Wrightson rural supplies store in Alexandra — I try to make up for the fact that I don't have much idea by having all the gear. One day when I was in there, Jared Manihera, one of their wool reps, hit me up about getting involved in a 24-hour shearing fund-raiser for the Southland Charity Hospital. It was hard to say no for a whole raft of different reasons. An old cobber, Dennis O'Connell, had already hit me up; it was a great cause; and I love spending time in shearing sheds when the job's on. I love how everyone rolls their sleeves up, mucks in and performs their role, almost without needing to communicate.

On Waitangi weekend 2022, half a dozen shearers would try to shear for 24 hours over a 32-hour period at Nelson and Fiona Hancox's Moa Flat farm in West Otago. It was a massive operation involving thousands of sheep, dozens of people — shearers, wool-handlers, cooks, sponsors, farmers, friends, family members — and two silly bastards on the microphone who were live-streaming around the world. The other fella on that mic was the South Island Heiniger rep, Willy McSkimming, a loose cannon who comes from shearing royalty. A very competent shearer himself, Willy knew how to talk shearing and both of us knew how to talk shit, so we had a bloody ball. It felt a bit like Willy was a brother from another mother.

You'd think shearers and wool-handlers doing the same thing over and over again for 24 hours would be a bit like watching paint dry, but those 32 hours flew by. I marvelled at the shearers — the way they handled the animals and placed their blows while maintaining an almost surreal level

Rura Support
TIME
FIRE EXIT
TOILET
ANZ
BAYLEYS
BDO

of intensity, sheep after sheep, hour after hour, into the night and beyond. For the shearers and wool-handlers it was about as hard as hard yakka gets, yet everyone was there for love, not money. It was Waitangi weekend and it was Māori and Pākehā coming together to do the mahi, without a cross word, without any animosity, without any problem. As everyone beavered away tirelessly, Willy and I asked for donations from the New Zealand public, and the New Zealand public donated. We raised more than $200,000 for the Southland Charity Hospital that weekend, and it was an absolute pleasure to be a small part of it. That's the sort of story we should see on the six o'clock news every Waitangi weekend.

After just a couple of hours' kip in the car, I drove home exhausted, but with new friends and new shearing connections. Jared and Willy turned up at Chatto Creek a few months later to shear my sheep before lambing. Initially we were just going to shear my Valais ewes, which have to be shorn twice a year, but in the end we did all the sheep on the property. Even though there's only about 100 of them, and Jared and Willy are gun shearers, it took us three days. At the end of the first day we decided we should shear the Southdown ewes the following day. At the end of the second day we decided to shear the rams the next. I think we were all enjoying each other's company so much we didn't want the job to end.

Stupidly, though, I forgot to organise some 'fadges' to put the wool in, so I just kept piling it on the back of the old ute, and then slowly drove it home while hoping it wouldn't fall off. I probably should've parked it in the garage, but didn't, so when the wind came up I had to pick up about a dozen different fleeces scattered all over the farm. By the time I collected up all the wool, put it into fadges and took it in to the local wool buyer, that was another day's work. If you didn't laugh, you'd cry.

Jared and Willy have been back a few times to shear my sheep and Willy, who lives in Ōamaru, sometimes stays the night. He's actually teaching me how to shear my sheep myself, which will be good because

Opposite Willy overseeing my work.

when he shears them, I want to pay him but he doesn't want to be paid, which can be awkward.

A year after the first 24-hour Shearathon I was involved in, we were back in West Otago doing it all again. I didn't think there was a chance of it being anywhere near as good as the first one, but it was. During the 2022 event, I'd jumped on the hand-piece and took the wool off about half a sheep. In 2023, after a few pointers from Willy, I was ready to shear a few of them. But there was a problem: I was far too confident. After a few lessons and having watched the professionals for hours, I thought I was a pro myself. I flew out of the blocks at about 100 k an hour, with wool, sweat and blood flying everywhere. Willy had to tell me to slow down as he sorted out a wound in front of a big, wide-eyed crowd. Sheep shearing would be one of the hardest things I've ever tried to do. That said, I still want to learn how to do it, and be competent enough to be able to do all mine on my own. Fortunately, I'll never have too many of them.

Sheep shearing would be one of the hardest things I've ever tried to do. That said, I still want to learn how to do it, and be competent enough to be able to do all mine on my own.

Another day I received a phone call from our builder, Dave Cockburn. 'Hey Matty, Chris Flannery's organising a golf day fund-raiser and wants you to speak at it — he's after your number.' The Flannerys are a reasonably famous sporting family from the Ida Valley. Even though I'd never met Chris, I certainly knew who he was and had heard he was battling cancer. After a quick chat on the blower, 'Flan' turned up on the farm.

'I hear you do a bit of public speaking — could you spin your yarn at our tradies and cockies golf day in Alex? We're raising money for Melanoma New Zealand.'

Opposite Willy McSkimming after a stint shearing.

Heiniger

Top: Willy and Jared shearing at my place. **Above**: Me and Chris Flannery at the fund-raiser where I spun yarns about him.
Photos from Matt's personal collection

Flan wanted me to talk about me at his event, but I had another idea. 'How about I talk about you instead?' I said to him. 'Give me the names and phone numbers of the ten most important people in your life; I'll interview them, and spin a yarn about you.'

Initially 'Flan Dog' was reluctant, but he eventually came around. I'd learn from his cobbers that Chris was more of a doer than a talker, a bloke who'd prefer the spotlight to be on someone else, a bloke who leads by example. He'd been really sick, but by the time the fund-raiser was coming round he was going pretty good. I put a lot of effort into interviewing Flan's top ten and I was probably given the best material I've ever had to work with. I think it was because he was on the up that his mates were prepared to put the boot in to him, good and proper. Even though I'd only spent about half an hour with Flan, I wanted to do a good job for him. His mates loved him like a brother and were finding it bloody hard to watch him and his family go through the pain they were going through. By the time I'd interviewed them all, I'd kind of fallen for Flan, too.

On the day, people turned up from all over the country to play golf, drink beer, talk rubbish and honour their mate, in the Alexandra sun. When it came time for me to talk, most of the people in the audience were reasonably plastered, and the dirt Flan's cobbers had dished up went down a treat. It could've been the best audience I've ever spoken to — they heckled, they jeered, they bent over laughing at 90-degree angles. It was kind of like Flan's funeral, only Flan was there, and that made it really special. He was able to laugh and be moved alongside everyone else, and I'm pretty sure he really appreciated it. He and his family thanked me profusely, and Flan has never stopped asking if I need a hand on the farm.

I always need a hand on the farm but I'm always reluctant to ask for it — well, I was right up until the spring of 2023. Because my sheep are so important to me, I couldn't handle lambing without keeping a watchful eye over them. As I was heading away on three work trips during lambing in October, I organised for someone to do a lambing beat for me — but at the last minute, because of unavoidable family reasons, they couldn't do it. By this stage I'd also agreed to speak at another of Flan's Melanoma New Zealand fund-raisers. It was time to call in a favour. I rang Flan, who was on the golf course, and put it to him; and without even knowing the details, he was in boots 'n' all. 'I'm good for lambing when needed. If you think I need a few hours with you beforehand, let me know.'

During my first work trip away, a set of lambs arrived stillborn but Flan was on the case. 'I got a lamb from Lindsay Scott and mothered it on. Strong lamb but Mum is not 100% accepting. I'll feed the lamb again at 7 tonight.' Flan named that lamb 'Scotty', after the guy he got him from, but we renamed him 'Flan'. When I came home from that trip I asked Flan if he enjoyed the farming, and he replied, 'Only if Scotty keeps feeding.' And he did. Flan (the human, not the sheep) was back on 'The Land' twice for my next two trips and I spoke at his next fund-raiser, and nothing screams community to me more than this little story.

In just these few years I've emcee'd a fund-raiser for a family doing it tough in Te Anau; I've emcee'd the Alexandra Blossom Festival; I've emcee'd Speed Shears at the Chatto Creek pub, and potato-growing competitions and auctions at the Ōmakau one. I've run with schoolkids who were running with a marathon runner in Ranfurly. I've had a 'night on the couch with Nadia Lim' to help the local ice-hockey kids get to Australia; that helped them raise thousands of dollars. I'm pretty sure I've done a whole lot of things I can't even remember doing. When I was up on stage at the local Blossom Festival I could barely see out of my eyes for tiredness. The day before, we were filming *Nadia's Farm* at Motatapu Station near Wānaka. When I got home I helped sort the kids, then spent hours doing a lambing beat till two in the morning. I flattened our wee car's battery sitting in it with the lights on and without the motor running. Then I got up at six to write a spiel for the Blossom Festival, went to the festival all day and half the night, and came home to go around my sheep again. Wouldn't not have done it, though.

Just this week I woke up in Ashburton to the phone ringing. It was my neighbour Robbo. 'We've got a problem. Have you got a black bull?

There's one in with my heifers.' Two hours later, the people at the Chatto Creek pub are posting about someone finding our dog on the rail trail. Tomorrow I really need to finish writing this book, but I'm on the mic at the 'Omakau Gallops' in Cromwell. The day after tomorrow I really need to finish writing this book, but I'm back in Ranfurly, judging a pie-making competition. Life, now, is a real juggle between heading away to earn money for work, doing work for love, and being a dad, husband and part-time farmer at home. I probably need to get better at saying no, but it's feel-good stuff that hopefully helps others. It definitely helps me.

Still, I often ask myself whether I'm making a big enough contribution in this world. But for one day at least, I stopped asking. I was dropping Bede off at school, not long after he started there. With a bag on his back that was almost as big as him, he high-fived me, kissed me on the lips and said, 'Love you Dad, you're the best dad in the world, thank you for everything you do for me.'

Then he jumped out of the ute and confidently walked across the field to his classroom. And when he was about halfway between me and the classroom he stopped, turned around and with his head held high, his school bag almost touching the ground he stood on, he raised his left hand, smiled and gave me a big thumbs up. And, rightly or wrongly, what I reckon Bede was saying to me in that moment was: 'Dad, you don't need to worry about me here, mate. I have absolutely got this — you've given me a good start, and I'm ready to give this education thing a real hiding.'

I drove away from Bede's school that day with tears in my eyes, and stopped worrying. For a while there I stopped questioning the contribution I was or wasn't making, and I just smiled and I cried.

FARMING FARK-UPS

THE LAND

I reckon the more you do in life, the greater the chance of things going wrong. There's always something to do on the farm, so you're always doing things, and so things are always going wrong — especially when I'm involved. I reckon when you're learning to farm in your forties, when you're just a part-timer and when you're maybe not as practical as you could be, there's an even greater chance of things going wrong.

I've always been almost sickeningly keen on my sheep, so distinguishing one from another is important to me. When I tagged my lambs in the very first year so I could tell who was who, the so-called permanent marker I used to number the tags wasn't actually permanent. So, I had to retag those lambs with a second lot of tags that had been numbered in a factory. Then, when I put in the much larger identification ear tags to 'ID' a sheep from a distance, I put them in the wrong place in their ear and they were unreadable. Fortunately, I got it right the fourth time.

'Hot' wires can be fun. At my place, for whatever reason, they're often not hot, and sometimes I just drive over them to get where I'm going. But one time the wire got caught up in the axle of the ute and it was wrapped around and around and around that axle real good. When I first tried to untangle the wire, what must've been about 9,000 volts pierced my body like a Northern Territory taipan and I soon remembered that my neighbour Pete had made that wire hot again the day before. Still, I stupidly chipped away for about half an hour, receiving more shocks than a depressed patient at Kingseat in the '60s, before realising I had the power to turn the power off by simply disconnecting the wire from the boundary fence. Not particularly effective electrotherapy in either case.

Another time, I had to return 400 metres of pipe I'd been using to run water to our house site so the tradies could build our dream pad. As I painfully pulled the pipe from the overgrown grass, I could see that the digger driver had separated what was two 200-hundred-metre lengths of pipe into about eight different pieces. Painstakingly I connected all that pipe back up again, then fumbled around rolling it into a couple of coils using Robbo's spinning jenny.

The harder I tried the more frustrated I became, and it didn't help that every time I stopped for a breather and to question my life choices, I could see the digger driver, who'd knocked the pipe into pieces in the first place, still working away.

After killing a couple of hours doing all of that, I still had a problem: I couldn't lift what was now a relatively awkward pile of pipe up on to the back of the ute. I changed from trying to pull the pipe up while standing on the back of the ute to trying to lift it up while standing on the ground, but it didn't matter whether I was pushing or pulling — I couldn't get that bloody pipe up on the back of the ute. The harder I tried the more frustrated I became, and it didn't help that every time I stopped for a breather and to question my life choices, I could see the digger driver, who'd knocked the pipe into pieces in the first place, still working away.

I texted Elle: 'If I had a gun right now, I'd use it.'

'You're suicidal over some pipe?' she replied.

In that moment, I was. It's often inanimate objects or 'process' that gets me in the end. Broken, hunched over, looking at my phone, I heard the digger driver's voice: 'Aren't you meant to be an advocate for asking for help?' And after struggling away for half an hour by myself, the two of us lifted that ungainly pipe on to the back of the ute in about five seconds.

Not long after I'd returned the pipe, we had another day I would rather not remember. The boys always want to ride on the back of the ute, and one Mother's Day I was driving around the land with the boys on the back of the ute. I usually make sure they're hanging on before I take off, but this one time, after stopping briefly to take a closer look at a sheep, I didn't. I'm still in first gear, a couple of seconds after slowly driving off, when Finn starts shrieking like he does when we take his iPad off him. Worried sick, I slam on the anchors, jump out of the vehicle, and run towards my four-year-old son. He's lying on the ground, bleeding from his head and crying uncontrollably. Crying so ferociously he can barely breathe. I locate the wound, stem the flow and wrap my arms around his fragile wee frame, but the tears keep coming.

I had whipped the boys away down to 'The Land' so that Elle could have a nice Mother's Day morning, but now I had to drive Finny home after falling off the back of the ute. I often feel awful, but I don't know whether I've ever felt much worse than I did at this moment. Understandably, Mum was both ropable and worried: 'Matt, you have to be so much more careful!' We drove Finn to see the urgent care doctor. She reckoned he was fine, but told us we should keep a close eye on him. Finn slept for a bit before we went out for what was meant to be a nice Mother's Day dinner at the reasonably flash 'Pitches Store' in Ophir. It was lovely, too, right up until Finn started vomiting his dinner back up.

Mum swept her salmon to the side. 'Matt, he'll be concussed, you need to take him to Dunstan Hospital.'

That was the end of the 'Thanks for everything you do, Mum' dinner. Fortunately, Finn *was* fine, but he and his guilt-ridden old man spent the night in hospital, having learnt a bloody good lesson.

IN OUR FOURTH WINTER HERE I had this great idea. I was wintering my cattle, and my breeding ewes and the hoggets that weren't in lamb, on this bloody terrible ryecorn stuff. But I wanted to look after my in-lamb ewe hoggets and ram hoggets a little better, so I had them in separate mobs on new grass, and I went and bought some more of those overpriced idiot bales of lucerne hay — which, while we're here, were stacked in former All Black Andrew Hore's shed. I'm just trying to impress you before I tell you how much of a halfwit I really am.

My two boys and I spontaneously left Chatto Creek late in the afternoon, borrowed a trailer about halfway there, in Ōtūrehua, and loaded up the old idiot bales in the Maniototo. After giving the old ute a real hiding chugging along the road for about an hour, we finally got back home. There's no hay barn at ours and we're in a high wind zone so the tarpaulin covering the hay often ends up 2 k down the road at the Chatto Creek pub. Not this year though, I'm too smart for that. This year, I did something that I thought had a touch of genius.

There's no hay barn at ours and we're in a high wind zone so the tarpaulin covering the hay often ends up 2 k down the road at the Chatto Creek pub.

In the dark, I singlehandedly unloaded 76 appropriately named idiot bales of lucerne hay into the garage of our brand-new, built in the pandemic, hugely overpriced home — and I did that without telling my wife. And *then*, I took to social media and posted a photo of my boys with the hay in the garage, saying: 'The boys and I are trying to figure out if putting the new hay in the new garage will be marriage-ending'.

Hundreds of comments came flooding in, ranging from 'funny' to 'not just marriage-ending, but potentially life-ending'. My wife wrote: 'Looks like you've made yourself a comfy bed', while my mother-in-law, Christine, wrote: 'The rats will move in to your beautiful new house . . . Also, if damp, can stain your concrete and can spread mould spores around your house and kids . . . eeeeek. And you do know hay heats up and can go on fire? Insurance??'

I replied: 'No, Christine, if I'd known that I wouldn't have done it'.

The lives of my beautiful little children — lives that give my life meaning when I sometimes struggle to find meaning — were at risk. So, at eleven o'clock at night, with my mother-in-law's words in my ear, I dragged my sorry arse out of the sack and loaded those well-handled idiot bales back on to the trailer and stacked them exactly where I'd stacked them the year before.

People, especially farmers, love hearing stories like these. They often tell me they've made most of these mistakes themselves. Usually, though, they're a lot more reticent that I am. For me, coming clean about almost everything has been really liberating.

LEARNING LESSONS

Spring can be such a glorious time of the year. After a relatively dormant winter, the sun comes out, the grass starts growing, the animals give birth and there isn't a whole lot that's more joyous than new life.

Spring is full of hope, but spring can also be brutal. After a reasonably tough lambing the previous year, I wanted to do everything I could to make things better in 2023. I wanted to turn the list of things I got wrong into a list of things I got right.

One of the first things on my 'to do' list was vaccinating the ewes against toxoplasmosis and campylobacter, which can cause abortion in sheep. I wasn't entirely sure whether or not my ewes had these diseases, but I do know I had lost lambs as soon as they were born and I know it was heart-breaking. I do a lot of googling, and Google told me I needed to vaccinate my sheep before I put my rams out. This year I decided to mate my ewes a couple of weeks later than usual, to try to avoid bad weather in September and also have a bit more feed on the ground for when the lambs were born. This would mean lambing at the start of October instead of mid-September.

My cobber Dan Thurlow, who's bought some of my Southdown rams three years running, messaged me to say he had some vaccine left over and did I want it. Of course I did, but the day he dropped it off I was heading out the door for work and didn't properly take in the vital information he was telling me. One of the vaccines was live, and I'd need to use it within the next couple of days. Of course I didn't, had to throw the vaccine away and would have to spend 350 bucks buying more. I also had to use one of the vaccines on the sheep twice, and I had no choice but to do one of these on a cold day in April when I had Covid. That day wasn't fun. It was probably the first day I questioned why I was farming. Regardless, even though I felt like a bag full of arseholes I got the job done and that gave me some peace of mind.

I reckon people think farmers are always complaining because farmers always have something to complain about.

It wouldn't be long before I was questioning my life choices again, and developing a real understanding of why people think farmers are always complaining. I reckon people think farmers are always complaining because farmers always have something to complain about. In the summer of 2022/2023 we were in a drought. The only thing that grew on the land we couldn't irrigate was thistles. In the end I had thistles that were taller than me, and they were that thick in places that it looked like I'd planted the buggers. Every time I went outside, I saw them. Every time I looked out the window, I saw them. On the land we were able to irrigate with k-line, the strong winds meant that at times the moisture was being sucked out of the ground as fast as we were putting the water on. I had to stop running — which keeps me healthy — because I didn't have enough time in the day because I had to move my k-line twice a day instead of once a day. I replaced my gumboots with sneakers so I could kill two birds with one stone and run while I moved the k-line. I didn't have to do it forever, though — at the point where you need the water the most, they limit your rations. In the end, we were only allowed to irrigate for 12 hours every second day.

We knew the rain would eventually come, but when it did it didn't stop. It seemed like every few days we'd get more rain. The grass that didn't grow in the drought started growing, and that brought its own problems. Long, wet grass wreaked havoc on my sheep's feet. I had twenty Swiss Valais Blacknose-cross sheep on new grass in front of the house and about thirteen of them started limping. Because they had wet, soft feet they developed scald, where the area between the hooves becomes inflamed and swollen. If untreated, scald can turn into footrot. I had two choices: do nothing and hope the lame sheep would somehow come right, or treat them. Most of my many farm advisers initially suggested I do nothing but pray. 'They should come right when we get a few frosts,' they said.

I did do nothing for a bit, but I couldn't do that forever. The limping got worse instead of better, and even though you can't look at a sheep's face and know it's in pain, I knew my lame sheep would be in pain. After a whole lot more googling and another post on social media, I came to believe that my best option was to run the sheep through a trough filled with a zinc sulphate solution. After treatment, the affected sheep would need to stand on a hard dry area for a day, but I didn't have a hard dry area. If I wanted to treat all of my sheep, which was about 100 of them in five different mobs, it would take me a week. A week that I didn't have.

After far too much thinking and inaction, I pencilled a day in my diary to do the worst mob — the Valais. I borrowed a plastic foot bath from the nearby town of Becks, bought a bag of zinc sulphate from PGG, and on that day pencilled in my diary I yarded my sheep. Depending on how you look at it, I probably couldn't have chosen a worse day to do the job. It was a white-out. A hoar frost with fog. Probably quite good for hardening the sheep's feet, but terrible for my morale. I mixed enough solution to fill the trough to the required level, but because the trough wasn't on level ground I didn't have enough solution in most of the trough. I had to head home and make some more. Then I wrestled one sheep at a time into the trough in the race, making sure it had all four hooves in that trough for the required two minutes. Initially I thought: 'Shit, it's annoying having to do this', but towards the end I started thinking how lucky I was to be able to do this on a weekday and tried to enjoy it.

I treated those twenty sheep three times that winter. While some lucky Kiwis might have been in Bali, or the Gold Coast, or Hawai'i, I was in Chatto Creek treating twenty sheep with scald, and 95% of those sheep eventually came right. It was hard to know whether they got better because of my intervention or not. Either way, I felt better for having done something rather than nothing, but I must admit to also thinking: 'I'm meant to be farming for fun and I don't know how much fun I'm having right now.' Farming is bloody hard yakka and I'm bloody sure you couldn't do it if you didn't love it. Fortunately, most of the time I do.

MY EWES WERE IN TERRIFIC condition when they went to the ram at the beginning of May. Actually, experienced sheep people might've said they were a little overweight. I used old JJ again on my 29 Southdown ewes with Merrydowns bloodlines, and his best son, the ribbon-winning 'The Land 202', on the seven ewes that weren't from Merrydowns. Just in case one of them was firing blanks, I swapped those rams over 31 days later. My purebred Swiss Valais Blacknose ram, 'Balmoral', ran with the nineteen Valais-cross ewes and the pet sheep Polly, and because I only had the one purebred Valais ram he had the mating duties all to himself, which was perhaps a little risky.

Because of the rain we had heaps of feed going into winter. My vet mate Dave Robertson reckoned that my 2022 lambs hadn't been big enough when they were born so some weren't strong enough to survive. I was determined that wouldn't happen again. Determined to feed my sheep better this winter so that my lambs were big enough and strong enough to survive whatever life threw at them when they popped out. I had half of my new grass 'shut up' for months to make sure it was available when needed.

I also had a paddock of ryecorn. Because grass hardly grows in winter, most farmers feed stock on crop they've grown through the spring, summer and autumn before. With crop, a lot of feed can be grown in a small area, allowing other parts of the farm to be rested. My sheep and cattle were all on grass right up until late June when I allowed them to have a crack at the ryecorn. Ryecorn is a cereal that grows well in dryland areas, but doesn't have much feed value. Apparently it tastes like shit, as I said before. When I first shifted the electric fences to allow my sheep to graze either the ryecorn or the old grass that they'd been grazing for weeks, it was pretty funny. They went over to the fresh new ryecorn and sniffed and tasted and peed on it, then turned around and beelined it for the old, worn-out grass. I thought: 'I'm in the shit here if these sheep won't eat this stuff.' I had to take away their option, fence off the grass and make them eat the ryecorn. Every morning for three months I moved two electric fences: for the first couple of months on the ryecorn, then on the new grass. If I had to go away for work, say for three days, I'd give them three days' worth of feed — and like kids with lollies they'd eat it all on the first day and then go hungry for two.

Initially I only had the sheep and cattle behind one electric fence, so when I went to move that fence the animals would often break out and tangle up the fence I was moving. It always seemed like there was a bigger mess to sort out on the days I had to catch a flight. Luckily, it didn't take long to figure out that if I put a second fence up behind the first one, the stock that broke out wouldn't have far to go. It was a life-changer. It's amazing how experience can make things easier.

Moving those electric fences most days was like medicine for me. I figured out the most efficient way of doing it, and would always take time to stop and appreciate the moment. I'd look at my healthy animals and listen to the contented sounds they made as they munched away on their breakfast. They were getting heaps of food, and that made me feel good. I never wanted to underfeed animals again. The plan was to have the cattle and the ewes on the new grass for another month, before spreading out the ewes in front of the house ten days ahead of lambing, which is pretty standard. This year I would try to avoid all the things I'd got wrong the previous year. This season I wouldn't underfeed my ewes, shear them just before lambing, lamb behind a wire, and lamb in a really exposed paddock.

But I was so focused on feeding my ewes well that I lost sight of the consequences of feeding them *too* well. About five weeks out from lambing, the ewe that had produced our award-winning ram lamb The Land 202, miscarried a set of twins. Two weeks later — just three weeks before the ewes were due to lamb — I noticed that a couple of them had bearings slipping in and out. This tends to occur in the last month before lambing, and while there is no single cause there are several factors that increase the risk. They're more common in highly prolific breeds and older sheep, as well as ewes that are fat and not getting enough exercise. Another risk factor is the 'feast or famine' scenario created by feeding sheep behind a wire.

I'd created the perfect storm. I had been overfeeding my older, highly prolific Southdowns too well behind a wire, and I was in trouble. I caught the two sheep with bearings and treated them with what's known as a 'retainer', but only one of them stayed in. Those two sheep were two of seven ewes that had been born on 'The Land' the first year we were down south and I was reasonably keen on them.

Ten days out from lambing I called my father-in-law. 'I start lambing in ten days — where do you think I should put my ewes next? I wanted to lamb in front of the house this year because it's a little more sheltered.'

'Jesus, Matt — you spread 'em out in there on all that new grass and you'll end up with half of your sheep popping bearings. Your sheep are too fat, you've been overfeeding them for months. They were too fat when you put your ram out, too. Well, the damage is done . . . but it'll be worse if you spread 'em out on that new grass. You could end up with about fifteen bearings.'

I was devastated. And I was worried. I'd caused a lot of problems the previous year by underfeeding my sheep, and now I was probably going to cause a lot of problems by overfeeding them. I changed my plans. I

2
2

spread my ewes out on older grass that had recently been grazed by my cattle, instead of the lush new stuff. About the same time, we got a couple of inches of rain. Almost immediately about ten of my big, fat, vulnerable ewes started hobbling around with sore feet. I was now worried about whether they'd be able to get around and eat enough tucker to feed them and their growing lambs. At this critical time, that could cause sleepy sickness or milk fever, which is fatal.

I caught the worst one, '846', treated her foot and gave her shots of penicillin and pain relief before having to go away for work. While I was away, a text came from Elle: '846, the ewe with the sore foot, is dead.' When I got home, I caught the ewe with the bad bearing and tried again to get the retainer working. But it wouldn't, and eventually I had to put her out of her misery. She had three big lambs in her belly. The same day she was euthanised — just a day before we were due to start lambing — I struggled to pull dead lambs out of another big sheep who was showing signs of lambing but wasn't interested in giving birth.

Halfway through, I pulled out my phone and messaged my sheep-breeding mate. 'Two dead. One more I can't get out. I'm done, Rob. I want to get out of sheep.' No matter what I did, I couldn't get that lamb out — and I knew that if I couldn't get it out and it was dead like its two siblings were, the ewe would die too. In that moment of desperation, having struggled away for what must've been close to an hour, I did something I've never done before. I cut the ewe's throat. I killed her and immediately cut her open to get that last lamb out, hoping it would be alive. But it was dead. If the neighbours had been home that late Friday afternoon, they would've heard some horrific language.

Three dead ewes out of 56 in a couple of days. I was absolutely over it. A house without any land in nearby Alexandra had never looked so good. Even Rob's reply didn't help much: 'It's always like this at the start. You'll be right.'

The next day, the first day we could realistically expect lambs — it was snowing. Great. I'd delayed putting my rams out to try to avoid bad weather in September, and now it was snowing. Fortunately, no lambs were born that day. I probably shouldn't be worried about national averages and what-not, but I'm constantly doing the maths — 'I've lost three ewes out of 56, so that's 5.35%. If I lose another three ewes I've lost more than 10% of my flock, and that's worse than average.'

With my father-in-law's voice still swirling around in my head, I was worried sick. Every time I checked the ewes I expected to see half a dozen new bearings. And when I was at home I checked those ewes about ten times a day. I had read that ewes are at greater risk of having bearings if they just sit around all day, so I would get up in their faces and force 'em up on to their feet. It seemed to work. The bearings didn't come.

Because of the change in plans, I'd shifted the cattle and rams into the slightly more sheltered paddock in front of the house. I wanted them to chew it out a bit, so that if I did decide to put the ewes in there for lambing they wouldn't have so much potentially bearing-producing tucker to eat. However, this came with its own problems. Our neighbour Robbo had recently told us to be careful with our new spring feed — Pete, the neighbour between us and him, had just lost a yearling heifer with bloat. The apparent cause was feed high in clover. I was back on the internet, googling 'how do you prevent bloat?', then off to PGG again to pick up a big bottle of bloat remedy. With just a few acres, you're always buying about ten times the amount of stuff you actually need. I was constantly going around my animals or staring out the window, looking for bloat or bearings. This problematic period immediately before the start of lambing is awful. The first live lamb never comes soon enough. It's always going to be a challenge, but I hope I eventually learn to enjoy it.

AFTER SOME REFLECTION, I EVENTUALLY calmed down. Compared with the year before, we were still looking pretty good. I feel awful sharing this, but in 2022 we went through ten ewes out of 67 before we got any live lambs. And this year, those live lambs did eventually come.

Just three days after my killing spree, I jumped out of the scratcher (bed) to find a healthy new set of Valais twins. *Finally*, we were away. The following day I helped a two-year-old Southdown give birth to a set of twins at half past ten at night. If I could bottle the feeling I had that night, I'd be happy for the rest of my life. Half a week after wanting to get out of the game, and I was back up on top of the world. I reckon lambing and calving are reasonably representative of farming in general: the lows are so low, the highs so high.

The live lambs kept coming, and they were strong — strong enough to handle the cold winds that had killed the smaller lambs at the start of lambing last year. I still wondered, though, whether I'd pay the price of having those strong new-born lambs — whether those bearings would still come. Every morning, I'd race out of bed to see what was going on; every night, I'd be out in the ute, watching and waiting.

Half a week after wanting to get out of the game, and I was back up on top of the world. I reckon lambing and calving are reasonably representative of farming in general: the lows are so low, the highs so high.

One Saturday morning the whole family came out to help me lamb a big old Southdown ewe who couldn't get the job done by herself. I pulled out one lamb, then I pulled out another, but the third lamb took a whole lot more effort. While I had its two front feet, I couldn't find its head. We got there eventually, but '311' wasn't as sprightly as her siblings and she wouldn't drink. It was going to be touch and go. I milked one of her mum's teats into a syringe and tube-fed the lamb to at least give her some life-giving colostrum. She was cold and being left behind by the rest of her family, and because Mum had three lambs and just two teats, the kids had their first pet lamb. My best mate 'Tuffers' and his two kids Max and Eva were staying on the weekend 311 was born. Once again, Max and Eva's

energy and curiosity reminded me that what's happening here on 'The Land' is really special. We named 311 'Mava' after Max and Eva.

A couple of days later, I pulled two big live lambs out of a ewe that had been struggling to birth overnight, but the ewe was dead within an hour. I used Flan's mothering-on technique and successfully got those two lambs feeding off 'Ears', a two-year-old pet, who'd lost a couple of her lambs. I later found out that no one tries to mother-on two lambs to a ewe, but I did. If I'd known that people usually don't try to do that, I wouldn't have tried. Just when you start thinking you've got this farming game sorted, though, something pops up to put you back in your place. Good old Ears fed those two lambs successfully for weeks before she went down with mastitis and we had another two lambs to bottle-feed.

Every night I'd be out in the ute, lights on, looking for action. I'd get to bed at eleven, twelve, one in the morning, then bounce out of bed at six for another look. Every second morning Bree would come too. She didn't really have a choice, but luckily she enjoys it. I'd get excited when the older Southdowns had triplets — great for the lambing percentage. As each lamb was born it would go into the diary and I'd crunch the numbers. Twenty-six Southdown lambs divided by twenty Southdown ewes equals 130%. For a while there I was looking like getting over 150% and I was tickled pink. But. Lambing percentage is actually calculated at tailing time, remember, and a lot of my lambs died before tailing. Even though their mothers were well-fed and the lambs were born a good size, so many of them didn't survive past three days. Again.

By the end of lambing, despite having supposedly sorted so many things from the previous year, I only had 40 Southdown lambs from 36 ewes mated. That was 111%. I was just 11% up on the previous year, which is exactly what Dennis had said we'd be. And while it was an improvement, I wanted more. My Valais lambed at 130%. I've figured out, though, that I'd been too forgiving. Often the ewes that didn't rear lambs last year didn't rear lambs this season either. I should have culled them, sent them to the freezing works, but I was too soft.

Dennis tells me I shouldn't be working out the lambing percentage during lambing, but I can't help myself. When I'm 'sitting the exam', I want to know how well I'm tracking. The thing is, though, this is all meant to be fun; something I do for me. Yet I treat it like a job. I probably take a lot of the fun out of it because I take it so god-damn seriously.

But, how can you not take it seriously when it's your passion and when lives are at stake? I wonder whether I will ever become accepting of death.

SHOW SEASON

OMAKAU

The A&P Shows, those good old-fashioned agricultural and pastoral shows, have always been a favourite day out for me. Being fond of people, fun and farming, each day is bloody near as good as you can get.

I've always harboured fond memories of going to the Tokomairiro A&P Show as a wee nipper in Milton. Wrapping my laughing gear around messy hot dogs dipped in sauce, chowing down on sticky pink candy floss, showing pet lambs, riding sheep, checking out all the animals and machinery on offer — for me, it was a celebration you didn't want to miss. Even when I was living in Auckland I went along to the huge Auckland shows and the Kumeū shows, and they were always a great reminder of where I'm from and where I wanted to end up.

A show is, however, always so much better when you know the people. The first year we were down south, we didn't film *Celebrity Treasure Island* because of the pandemic so I was able to head along to the local Central Otago show in Ōmakau with my family. At that stage Bede was three and Finn would have been nearly two. We'd only been living in the area for a few months, so it was going to be a great chance to catch up with people. Even though we were new to the area, by now we'd been holidaying here for half a dozen years, and I'd also gone to school and university and played footy with or against a lot of the locals.

I was also asked to join rural personality and steady pair of hands Sarah Perriam on the mic. Crikey it was busy, and I was terribly torn. Finn or Bede would want to chat to me about something — probably to ask for money — but I'd be in the middle of commentating a sack race or an egg-and-spoon race or whatever. While I loved it, it wasn't easy trying to be a dad, a commentator, a local, and actually do what I wanted to do all at the same time. All that said, we got through it. I didn't need to worry about the Broadcasting Standards Authority so was able to push the boat out, be a little naughty and make people laugh. One of my favourite things to do is make people laugh.

It was a bloody good show, too, for the size of the community, and I remember thinking: *What a great event, what a great community, what a great place to live.* And thinking: *This is what we've come here for.* It was so good to be mixing with our clan again. I never want any day like that to end. Even though I don't drink nowadays I still don't want to go home, though as a father of young children you have to.

It was a bloody good show, too, for the size of the community, and I remember thinking: *What a great event, what a great community, what a great place to live.*

A few weeks later I was a special guest of the Mt Benger show in Roxburgh, just down the road. It was more of the same, and it was brilliant. I actually think I got third in the 'women's' agri-sports competition. My parents lived in Roxburgh before I was born, and people never forget. The old idiot box is also a good ice-breaker: 'So, what's Mike Hosking *really* like?'

As good as those shows were, though, they wouldn't compare to the 2023 show season. By then I'd been axed from *Celebrity Treasure Island*, but every cloud has a silver lining. It meant *not* being away from home for weeks on end while we filmed. Finally, I could show my stud Southdown sheep at a show.

The previous season I'd increased the size of my flock by about 350%, going from eleven to 38 ewes going to the ram. That ram, JJ, was supposedly a ripper, a real gift; plus, the new ewes had come from Merrydowns. I thought even I couldn't stuff this up. There was a good chance I'd produce some decent lambs, and I did reckon some of them were pretty good. As usual, due to ignorance, I didn't enter the Ōmakau show in time but got around that after having a nice conversation with someone. With their help, I entered two individual ram lambs, a pair of ram lambs, two individual ewe lambs, old JJ himself, a home-bred two-tooth ewe, and an older Merrydowns ewe.

Another thing I didn't know was that entering those sheep in the show would take up a good chunk of the bloody week. First, the rams needed to be tested for brucellosis, a bacterial disease that permanently infects the testicles and epididymis of rams, leaving them infertile. The last thing any ram breeder would want was a whole lot of really good stud rams that they couldn't sell because that lifestyler Matt Chisholm had brought his disease-ridden, infertile rams to the show and now everyone's rams were firing blanks. I was late getting to the testing, which is typical when you're a part-timer and you're not terribly well organised. I probably rang the vet about Monday or Tuesday before the show on Saturday, asking whether someone could test my rams.

'Yep, if you can get them yarded on Wednesday, we can test them that afternoon and get the results back by Friday, so you can take 'em to the show Saturday.' It was going to be tight, but it was going to work. So on Wednesday morning, I slowly but surely got those rams yarded. The vet turned up on cue that afternoon, took some bloods and then took those bloods away with him. By the time I had the rams back where they belonged, Wednesday was about done.

On Thursday I went down to the local domain to help set up the sheep pens for the show. By the time we'd finished doing that, and a burger and Coke at the local boozer, that day was about done, too. Then on Friday, I had to get all the sheep back in to sort 'em ready for the show. Remember, I was taking both ewes and rams, and for around eleven months of the year you don't keep them together, so they had to be got in from all over the place. I now started to worry about how the vets were getting on with my brucellosis results. I rang them.

'Sorry, Matt, but I don't think we're going to get them back in time.'

I was horrified. 'But, mate — you said we would . . . I've already got the bill for 200-odd dollars and there's no point testing the rams if I don't get the results before the show. I only wanted them tested so I could take them to the show.'

It didn't matter what I said, they couldn't do anything. I wouldn't know if my rams had the awful brucellosis before the show or not.

Would I be ballsy enough to take my rams to the show without knowing their brucellosis status? I asked another breeder. 'You'll be fine, mate,' he said. 'They won't have it and I'm bloody sure no one will ask.' Taking that risk really didn't feel right, but I'd been wanting to take my sheep to the local show for three long years. After a little bit more research, I decided to take the risk. Fingers firmly crossed.

A MATE OF MINE FROM Southland, Rob Hall, who was also showing his Southdown sheep at the show, came and stayed with us on the Friday night. It was a good catch-up and an exciting time. We were out of the sack early, full of anticipation, getting our sheep out of my father-in-law's yards and off to the show. But when we got there, I wasn't sure whether I should take my sheep off the trailer. Would they be good enough to be shown? Would I disgrace both myself and the breed?

We waited patiently, me anxiously, while people in front of us backed their trailers flawlessly and unloaded their sheep. Then the other local Southdown breeder, Donny Maclean, walked past and said, 'Are those your

Southdowns? They look bloody good.' It was just what I needed to hear. We got 'em off the trailer, penned 'em up, and then Rob trimmed them up a little bit with a set of shears. The judging started. Rob, Donny and I were all going head to head with the Southdowns. The others had been breeding Southdowns for decades; I'd been at it for just three years.

While some other blokes were sorting out the men from the boys with the Southdowns, as a steward I was 'helping' to judge the Suffolks; part of trying to learn as much as I could about sheep. It was a nervous time focusing on the Suffolks, all the while wondering how well my Southdowns were doing (and whether or not my rams were full of a disease that could ruin everyone else's sheep). The anxiety was broken by smoko, and a chance to make some new friends — real farmers who were generally stoked that I was having a red-hot go. After a cuppa and some cake it was back to the judging and it didn't take long to clean the rest of them up.

How well had my Southdowns actually done? I beelined it for my small pens of sheep just like the kids going for cotton candy around the corner, and saw certificates hanging from the weathered gates. With just three breeders in the race, though, the presence of certificates meant nothing — everyone would get one. It was the *colour* on the certificate that was important: yellow for third, blue for second, red for first. My best older ewe, 'Merrydowns 395', only got third. My huge Tahrua ram, JJ, had a blue certificate — second. So did my second-best ewe lamb, 'The Land 211', and my second-best ram lamb, 'The Land 224'. But who'd beaten those lambs? Donny's or Rob's? It was *mine*. The judges reckoned I had the best ram lamb. I had the best *pair* of ram lambs. And I had the best ewe lamb. *And* — I had the best two-tooth ewe.

It might sound ridiculous, but that was one of the coolest moments of my life. Having dreamt about having a wee farm for more than 40 years, and then having had such a rough start to lambing where I seemed to make about half a dozen fatal mistakes, I had actually bred, and fed, some really good sheep. It was promising and it was encouraging and it was glorious and I was just so grateful.

As usual, though, I couldn't help but focus on the negative, and asked the judges why old JJ hadn't won. 'Oh, he probably wasn't quite right on his feet. Your ram lamb though — The Land 202 — keep feeding him. He's a bloody tremendous sheep.' I knew he was a ripper, built like Mike Tyson, but I also knew the results came down to the opinions of just two judges.

I put my sheep to the test again at Ōamaru's North Otago show and at Invercargill's Southland show, where I had a job on the mic. I wasn't keen on the effort involved in getting your sheep to a show — getting them in, sorting them, loading them and transporting them — and I don't have a trailer, but when Dave Robertson asked if I'd bring my sheep to Ōamaru it was hard to say no. The boys and I could go and catch up with their grandma; kids can never see enough of their grandparents. Also, I now knew that my rams were brucellosis-free (and I can't tell you how good it felt to dodge that bullet). On top of that, if I took my sheep to Ōamaru my vet bill for the brucellosis test was going to be effectively halved. Cut into thirds, if I took them to Southland as well.

So, off we went with slightly fewer sheep than I'd taken to Ōmakau, and left them camping up at Dave's on the Friday night. The kids were still in bed at Grandma's when I took off back to Dave's on the Saturday morning. I always allow myself plenty of time for any farm job because I always plan for the worst-case scenario. When I arrived at Dave's, on the outskirts of Ōamaru, he was already out in his yards. My sheep were in the same set of yards so I could easily compare our stock and, rightly or wrongly, I thought Dave's looked better than mine. He busted out a small pair of blades and began trimming the wool on some of their faces. Southdowns often have woolly faces, which I quite like, but obviously Dave doesn't. My sheep would go au naturale. They'd be going toe to toe with Dave's sheep and Chris Medlicott's Southdowns from Clifton Downs. Both these blokes are particularly good operators and I'd be happy getting third. Although, when there are just three people playing the game, getting third means coming last.

Ōamaru was even busier than Ōmakau had been. I was showing

my sheep, trying to hang with Bede and Finn who both had 20 bucks burning holes in their pockets, and with Mum and, later, my brother Nick, sister-in-law Nicola, and their triplets Rubi-Soo, Dakota and Loki, who'd turned up from Dunedin. In different ways, Nick and I had both been on national telly for fifteen years and now we were back at our old high-school stomping ground. We couldn't move 10 metres without bumping into someone who wanted a yarn. Bede and Finn would be pulling my left hand towards some kind of carny-like stall and I'd be shaking hands with someone with my right. It was chaotic, yet beautiful at the same time. I sensed that the locals were happy to see us, they seemed proud of us; and when I finally got a moment to think, I was proud of us, too. Nick, who is a quadriplegic, was there with his beautiful little family. I, with my boys and my sheep, was finally doing what I really wanted to do. And our gorgeous wee mum who, after watching her two youngest boys struggle through different chapters of their lives, was right there in the thick of it; probably more proud than anyone. She never once missed an opportunity to introduce her sons, or her grandchildren, or let people know we'd been on television or were sober or something similar. We were that bloody busy, we didn't eat lunch till afternoon tea time.

I sensed that the locals were happy to see us, they seemed proud of us; and when I finally got a moment to think, I was proud of us, too.

But: how did my sheep go against Dave's and Chris's — the local guns?

Pretty bloody well, actually. My home-bred two-tooth ewe The Land 102 and my best ram lamb The Land 202 were both judged second — while my best ewe lamb The Land 206 came first. Chris cleaned up with most of the other prizes. I was rapt, but felt for Dave, who seemed a little dejected. I'm pretty sure he was marked down for trimming the faces of some of his sheep.

SOUTHDOWN BREEDER ROB HALL IS a very proactive and passionate A&P Show man — bit of a dying breed these days. I'm pretty sure he put some pressure on me to take my sheep south: 'I've taken my Southdowns to Ōmakau, buddy, so you better bring yours to Invercargill.' Regardless, because I had a paid gig on the mic so would be driving south anyway, it made sense to take my sheep. The week leading up to the event, I was on a Southland radio show and joked about how I'd won certificates in Ōmakau and Ōamaru and was now chasing ribbons in Invercargill. Okay, I was joking about wanting ribbons, but I seriously wanted those ribbons.

Unsurprisingly, it was a drizzly old autumn day in the Deep South on show day, but it didn't stop the punters from turning up and enjoying themselves. I co-hosted with Rob's sister, Margs Hall, who is as passionate about stock as Rob; we spent a fair chunk of time talking turkey — talking sheep and cattle. Margs was really competent on the mic and took control of the basics, which allowed me to clown around and have fun. I can't remember now whether I beat Rob in the hobby-horse race or he beat me, but I do remember what happened with the sheep. First, Rob took heaps of Southdowns to Invercargill and won a special cup for winning the most points out of any Southdown breeder on the day. I couldn't have been any happier for him, but I'd actually thought I'd be the one taking the cup home. And the reason? I'd nabbed more certificates than a kid starting out at school. The lambs I produced the previous year really cleaned up. As well as that, my home-bred, nearly two-year-old ewe The Land 102 came first. The judges also reckoned I had the best pair of Southdown ram lambs. The Land 206, which had won in both Ōmakau and Ōamaru, was again the best Southdown ewe lamb and, this time, the best Southdown female at the show.

I had nabbed my first ribbon, but my prize ram lamb The Land 202 would go one better. He was judged the best Southdown ram lamb, champion Southdown ram, and Supreme Champion Southdown. Unbelievable. The judges thought I had the best ewe and ram out of all 37 Southdowns at the Southland A&P Show. I was tickled pink. I would

Top: Members of my family at the North Otago show.
Above: Celebrating at the Southland show with my prize ram lamb The Land 202. *Photos from Matt's personal collection*

have been happy to have just shown some sheep that didn't disgrace me and the breed. I was happy just being a part of it all; showing some solidarity with rural New Zealand. But this!

I drove home from the show that Saturday night with seven certificates, three ribbons, and a smile wrapped right across my face for the entire two-and-a-half-hour journey. On the way I stopped for a feed in Gore and ran into Blair Robertson's son, Jack, at the pub. Blair's the bloke I'd bought the majority of my ewes from. A good bugger. I texted him to tell him I'd run into his young fella at the boozer, but of course it was really just a conversation-starter so I could let him know that this new breeder, out of Auckland of all places, had done okay with his ewes.

The move south to the country had never felt so good. It's the wee wins like this that keep me going.

A DOG'S LIFE

SKELLERUP
RED BAND

Ever since I lost my beautiful sheepdog Rock when I was a kid, I've wanted to replace him. When we moved to the country at the end of 2019, we took one step closer to doing that.

Now, I go around my sheep and cattle so much that they've become really tame, which makes them difficult to move. I'm also my mother's son and a bit of a 'feeder', so my sheep and cattle have been overfed and this also makes them difficult to move. With well-fed, tame stock you can get right up to them and give them a pat or a scratch, which is pretty cool. Of course there's a flip side. Because we don't yet have any sheep or cattle yards on our place, every time I need to get my sheep and cattle in to handle them, which often happens with the sheep especially, I have to take them off our farm and up the hill to my father-in-law's yards. It's 300 metres from the top of our place or a kilometre from the bottom. Moving fat, tame stock without a dog, especially in the height of summer, can take forever.

To move them in the right direction, I follow them in the ute, yelling, tooting and slapping the door. When all of that stops working, I slam on the hand-brake, jump out of the vehicle and zigzag around behind the animals like a dog. It's good for my fitness but terrible for morale. I didn't have to do this too often before realising I needed a dog.

Dogs are worth their weight in gold down on the farm, but they also need a heap of work and I don't really have enough time to give them. What I needed was a loyal old dog who could see out its final years on 'The Land', do a bit of work here and there, and be an awesome family pet. A dog just like the one I'd grown up with as a kid. All I wanted was an old black-and-tan huntaway just like Rock.

I put a post out on social media, and within a week got a dozen replies with offers from Canterbury to the Catlins. While most of the dogs had four legs, at least one just had the three. None of the offers, though, seemed quite right. While I'm getting better the older I get, annoyingly I'm still the kind of guy who likes things *just right* and I had my heart set on a Rock Mark II. About a fortnight after the post, though, I received a message from George Naylor, a good young farming fella in our valley, who I've talked with quite a lot. 'How are you getting on finding a dog, Herb? I think I might have the perfect old boy for ya.'

'Shade' or 'Shadey Pup' was a beautiful-natured nine-year-old brown-and-tan huntaway who had been a brilliant working dog but was now a little long in the tooth to handle full-time farm work. I drove out to George's as soon as I could for a look, and even though Shade wasn't quite the right colour he was gorgeous and friendly, and perfect. All he needed to do now was bark and he would pass the interview. George briefly sent Shade out around a mob of sheep, and he listened, ran and barked beautifully before being called back to his boss.

'That'll do 'im,' said George. 'I don't want to work 'im too hard.'

'He looks like a bloody ripper, but what are his commands?' I asked.

'You won't need 'em,' said George. 'He'll work on autopilot — he's been doing it that long he knows what to do.'

I asked him how much he wanted for Shade. 'Nothing, mate, we just want him to go to a good home.' George was obviously still attached to his old dog, so I immediately whipped 'Shadey Pup' back to our rental in Ōmakau before he could change his mind.

Everyone fell for the old fella straight away; well, almost everyone. When we first got him home he used to bark at night, which upset at least one of our neighbours. Every day I was at home, Shade and I would make the five-minute journey down to 'The Land' together. One of us was really experienced, the other really inexperienced, but we were equally as excited as each other. Unfortunately, anticipating what was to come, Shade would bark the whole way there. Unfortunately, if I'm honest, once there, neither of us really had that much to do. Shade soon became more of a mate than anything else. Most of the time he would just lope about doing dog things — the looking, the sniffing, the scratching and the peeing. After he'd cased the joint out again, he'd sidle up to me, rub himself against my legs and start nuzzling away at my hands, asking for a pat. He had the most beautiful soft coat and ears. I loved playing with his ears; there was comfort in it. He loved me playing with his ears, too.

Ninety per cent of the time, old Shade was great for morale. We were great cobbers and I loved him, but unfortunately my new best mate wasn't actually that helpful with the stock. Sure he'd bark at the cattle, but those cows must've known he was old and tired. As soon as he started barking at them, chasing them, they'd turn around and chase him back. He would briefly give my fat sheep a bit of a hurry-up. But just briefly. The poor old bugger would only last about ten minutes before he was cooked and had to lie down, panting for breath. On a hot summer's day that ten minutes could be just five. I'd have to carry on without him or pick him up and have him ride shotgun in the air-conditioned cab. My father-in-law Dennis was the first to suspect he might have had a stroke at some point.

Fortunately for Shade, he was a beautiful old bugger and a great mate. The relationship between a man and his dog can be amazing, can't it? I do have to say, though, that amazing relationship was always tested when Shade had to give up halfway through a job. He'd often be parked up in the wrong place, still barking, pushing the sheep in the opposite direction to where they needed to go. But we had to keep taking Shade out to work because Shade always wanted to go.

One hot day in January, the boys, Shade and I had to muster the sheep into the yards, but a few minutes in, Shade pulled the pin. As we weren't far from home, and water, we left him to it, expecting to meet him back at the house when we'd finished the job, like we often did. But when we got home, Shade wasn't there. Worried, I left the boys and beelined it for where we'd last seen him. And there he was, lying peacefully. Still. Gone. Our beautiful old boy, now covered in thousands of small flies. I furiously swiped them away from his already stiff body as tears rolled down my face.

Although it was far too soon, it was the end I'd wanted for my mate, a mate we'd had for just fourteen months. Shade had died doing what he loved. He'd died on the job. It really hurt, but the hardest part was yet to come. I had to break the news to Elle and the boys, and to Shade's old owner who loved him as much as, if not more than, we did. I wrapped my arms around Shade like I'd done so many times before, put him in the ute and drove him home to the family. Then I rang George, who was as heartbroken as the rest of us. We all wept as we dug his grave — a grave with a great view over the land he'd worked, looking south down to Alexandra. We then buried our buddy and adorned his grave with flowers, kids' drawings, and more tears.

A few days later, I received a message from George. 'Hey, I've got a new litter of black-and-tan huntaway pups on the ground. They'll be great dogs, 'cos their mum and dad are beauts. I'd love for you to have one, mate. I can get 'im started for you — whadaya reckon?'

We all wanted this one friendly wee fella with a scar on his back, because we all love an underdog in our house.

We were excited once more; still sad for Shade, but excited nonetheless. The next spare day we had, the whole family was back at George's to choose a pup. We all wanted this one friendly wee fella with a scar on his back, because we all love an underdog in our house. He looked just like

Rock had 40 years ago. He was too young to come home yet, so we left him where he was and spent the entire trip home trying to figure out what we'd call him. And then, as we drove up our drive, Bede said, 'Rock. We should call him Rock, Dad.' No other name could come close. Forty years after I'd had a black-and-tan huntaway called Rock, we had a black-and-tan huntaway called Rock.

Walking a dog in paradise turns out to be bloody good therapy.

We picked him up a few weeks later, and I've been worried about having to train him ever since. Just like Shade, and the Rock he was named after, Rock II has a great nature. But at nine months old he's a little annoying; not so much for me but for everyone else. He's a shoe-stealer and he jumps up on people. I can get him to sit, though, and when I yell 'Wallago', he comes back to me. When I yell 'Inside', he'll go into his kennel. At the moment he's turning expensive food into dog poo, but I'm really looking forward to having some time to train him. We need to be starting to do that about now. I've already enlisted the help of local legend and keen dog trialist Bill Hinchey, who lives just over the road here in Chatto Creek. Bill reckons he's showing a lot of potential. 'But then,' he said, 'most dogs show a lot of potential.'

Time will tell. In the meantime, I've found that one of the best things I can do when I'm feeling a little blue is let Rock out for a bit. Walking a dog in paradise turns out to be bloody good therapy.

Opposite Chatto Creek's Bill Hinchey with a young pup.

THE STATE OF PLAY

We've been south for nearly four years now. We're really only just starting out. It's late spring. A Sunday. The temperature must be mid-20s. I've fed the seven pet lambs. And the dog. And the two pigs. One of them, the biggest one, looks unhappy; she's off her tucker. I wonder whether, after feeding her for five months, she'll die before we get to eat her, and it plays on my mind. The boys and I have just helped Nana next door move some cattle, while Grandad rests up after a hip operation. We've walked through their almost completed new house, just over the fence from ours. Now, while I'm tapping away on the computer, the boys are busy watching a drawing lesson on the iPad. I can hear an annoying American voice in the background. Elle's tidying the house. Bree's following her around with a brush and half-shovel: 'Mumma? Can I help, Mumma?' There are toys scattered everywhere. Two shoes here. One over there.

I need to write another 2,500 words for the day. I need to feed the seven pet lambs again. A glance outside reminds me of how much else there is to do. The new lawn is coming on slowly. It needs water. It's patchy; imperfect. The lawn is separated from the farm by an electric fence; this temporary fence will become a permanent one when money comes. If it comes. Now, I'm understocked — I can barely see my sheep for the long grass that's going to seed. You don't want your grass to go to seed because it loses its feed value. Three people have pointed this out to me in the past 24 hours, probably because they think I don't know. We've got so much feed we're actually sharing it with the neighbours, while they save theirs for winter.

We *are* chipping away on our wish list, but it's still long and expensive. You tick two things off, add another one on. The list of hiccups in the past few weeks alone tells that story pretty well. We had to spend more than $2,000 cutting and baling some ryecorn I was talked into planting, because in late spring it was starting to go to seed and the animals apparently won't eat it then. The contractor thought it would cost about $50 a bale to produce about 30 bales of ryecorn. When the first bill came in, though, we'd been charged $72 a bale. We could only sell it for about $60 a bale, so we'd lose $12 on each bale on top of the cost to produce the wretched ryecorn in the first place.

Days after that baleage was neatly placed on our boundary, five-year-old Finn took a large knife to it, slashing at least half of the bales, which took a couple of hours to patch. And just a couple of weeks after that, the ryecorn that was still in the ground shot away so quickly that it went to seed. So we'd dropped two grand to avoid a plant from going to seed, but it went to seed anyway. Now we probably have to spend more money spraying the supposedly inedible seedy, stalky ryecorn and plant something else in its place. The upside is that we've got 32 bales of ryecorn baleage that our cattle might eat in the winter.

Using an electric fence, we tried to get some of my father-in-law's cattle to eat that seedy, stalky ryecorn, but the electric fence unit broke, the cattle busted out, and one of Dennis's bulls jumped the boundary fence and had his way with Robbo's young cows. So, late at night, I had to shift those bulls and cows from that paddock, and while I did that they made a real mess of the no-longer-hot electric fence that I hadn't had time to take down. A few days after that we got a water leak just as the summer heat hit, so to ensure that a different mob of cattle had water, I moved them, too. And they also got tangled up in that same no-longer-hot electric fence, which ended up strewn all over that shitty paddock of seedy, stalky ryecorn.

About the same time that Dennis's Angus bull jumped the fence, our Highland bull Hamish did the same thing on our place, ruining a gate as well as a few beasts we hadn't wanted him to impregnate.

All our grass has gone to seed, too. I can't 'top' it because I don't have a tractor or a topper, and if I did have a tractor and a topper I still couldn't top a lot of it because I hadn't rolled it first as I didn't have the money to pay someone to do it. You roll land to push any stones back into the ground so that they don't ruin blades when topping or mowing.

We're still feeding pet lambs three times a day, which is both good and bad. It's bad because it takes up time I don't have, but it's good because it gets me out looking at the sheep, which usually makes me feel good. But lately, it hasn't made me feel so good. I've noticed a couple of ewes twitching at their rear ends, so I've caught them and confirmed my worst fears. Maggots. I've had to go back to the house, grab some blades and the stuff you use to treat flystrike, then go and catch those sheep for the second time and treat them. Meanwhile, the lambs need tailing, the ewes need to be shorn, the calves need to be castrated and I need a holiday. I'll get one soon, though, and I can't wait.

YOU SEE, A MONTH OR two back I was feeling burnt out all over again; the signs were everywhere. I'd come home from being away for a few days, with a 'to do' list as long as my arm. There was always some job to do, but what I wanted, and needed, to do was have an afternoon with my kids in the swimming pool. Instead I was sitting at our large living-room table, tapping away on my computer, when one of Elle's friends arrived. We didn't know she was coming and Rock, our untrained huntaway pup, was out of his kennel having a runaround. Rock's a little too 'jumpy uppy' at the moment; I can kind of handle him but often others can't. So Rock was jumping up on Elle's friend, and then he started jumping up on Elle, who spilt her coffee all over the floor and then started barking at me. 'You really need to sort out this bloody dog, Matt.'

And Elle was 100% correct. I did need to sort out the dog, but I've never trained a sheepdog before and right then I didn't have time. I also needed to lamb my ewes, contain my cattle, put in the new lawn, pay our huge mortgage (which means writing this book), direct a TV show, fly around the country as the inaugural ambassador for the Rural Support Trust, and generally say yes to anyone else who wants me to do something for them. I'd been going hard at it for months and was struggling to do all of these things, and when my wife said — in front of our visitor — 'You really need to sort out this bloody dog, Matt', I snapped.

'When the *hell* do you expect me to train the bloody dog, Elle? I have this long list of things to do, and training this bloody dog is about number 37 on that bloody list of things to do.'

Later I apologised to our visitor, and to Elle. It wasn't about the dog. It was about where I was at, trying to keep the wolves from our door. Travelling all over the country to work hard to pay a big mortgage on our 'farm' — which doesn't make any money — then, at home, always having something to do on the 'farm'.

Of course, every time I'm away from home Elle has to take care of the kids, and the farm, by herself. We have created an unbelievably busy life for ourselves. Like I said, we're busier than we've ever been before.

Farming's a tough gig. It feels like you're always battling with something; always trying to put out fires. Farming never, ever stops. There's always something to do, and often you have to do that something when you're meant to be doing something else. The cattle break out when you're off to a barbecue, or when you're in a different part of the country. Perfect isn't a word down on the farm. No matter what conditions you're facing, there's always a negative. It's Mother Nature letting you know she's still in charge. If you don't get enough rain, the grass doesn't grow. If you get too much rain, your sheep get bad feet. And farmers are price-takers.

RED BAND

One season I got $300 for cull ewes. The following year I only got 75. One year it's $175 for my lambs, the next 125 — for basically the same animals, in the same condition, just with different ear tags. For real farmers, that means they don't make any money that season. They work 70, 80, 90 hours a week, and don't make any money.

You can't spend time and money doing riparian planting if you haven't got any money. You can't go green if you're not in the black.

While I'm obviously no expert, I reckon the business model for farming is a little broken. Real farmers have to spend millions of dollars buying land, stock and plant, so they can go farming, and some years they don't make any money. On top of that, everyone wants to have their say on how farmers should farm, even if they don't know very much about farming. A lot of people don't want farmers to use sprays, or fertilisers, or water, but for a lot of farmers, if they didn't use those things their farms wouldn't be economically viable. If farmers can't make a profit, they'll go out of farming. You can't spend time and money doing riparian planting if you haven't got any money. You can't go green if you're not in the black.

I went to university with hundreds of people who studied farming. Twenty-five years on, most of them are doing something else. They've become plumbers or pilots or physiotherapists. Older farmers are telling their children to do something else with their lives. They don't want to see their sons and daughters indebted up to their eyeballs. Young farmers might have to borrow about five million dollars to go farming, and when interest rates are high that's a big noose around your neck. And then a whole lot of people dislike you because you're all greedy environmental vandals, ruining the planet. But here's the rub: many of those people pointing the finger at the farmers are flying to Hawai'i for their holidays. And people don't *need* to fly to Hawai'i for their holidays, but they do need to eat.

I'm actually really worried about who is going to farm the land in the future. The rest of us are only able to work as journalists and doctors and builders and everything else because farmers produce the food. If we make it too hard for them, no one will do it. Me aside, the overwhelming majority of Kiwi farmers are really good at it. We produce food and fibre really efficiently and sustainably in this country. A lot of New Zealand farmers are already doing so many of the things all the non-farmers want them to be doing, before they're forced to do them. I reckon that if we're really concerned about looking after the planet, New Zealand should be farming more, not less. If we produce less, the slack will more than likely be taken up by less-efficient and less-sustainable producers from elsewhere in the world, and that would be worse for the planet.

FOR ME, AS HARD AS it's been at times, I feel really fortunate and privileged to have been able to get a real insight into the reality of farming.

Sure, going country has been hard. Starting anything is hard. And of course farming is hard. Life after the pandemic is hard. Life is hard for a lot of people. I actually think life is easier when you figure out it's hard; I hope that makes sense.

But going country has also been beautiful, and healthy, and wholesome, and rewarding. It's been a dream come true, and in realising that dream I'm terribly lucky. I liken life on the land to a life on drugs. The highs and lows are bigger than usual. You feel the cold more because you're out amongst it. You feel the heat more because you're out amongst it. We're so dependent on the weather and on nature, and nature can fill your cup and break your heart on the same day. But nature also makes me feel a whole lot more human. Nature is the best drug I've ever used. We'll never make any money 'farming' on the scale we do, but it doesn't matter. For me, this is living. This is the life I want to live, even if it isn't easy.

Lately, there's also been some change on the wish-list front and there's a lot to look forward to. I've just received a message from an old university footy mate, Fraser Fletcher, who farms just down the road in Heriot, West Otago. I'm told he's farming in a big way and he's a good operator. We talk farming via online messaging at night when I've forgotten to get myself to bed early.

Today's message went: 'Truck's here at 6am in the morning. Dick will ring later for drop off details.' Fraser and I have talked for months about him sending me some of his stud Shorthorn cattle, and finally a few are coming. And Dick Knight — the former Otago footy player who used to drive me down to the Clutha sale from Milton when I was seven — is bringing them, 40 years on. Amazing.

There could be about twenty Shorthorn cows roaming 'The Land' by March, and I'm bloody excited about it. To me, Shorthorns are the Southdowns cattle. The oldest pedigree cattle in the world, they come in three colours — white, red and roan — and have helped form about 40 new cattle breeds. I've done heaps of research. Asked dozens of people about them. Most farmers nowadays have Angus or Hereford cattle because their breeders have done a brilliant job of marketing them. (Think McDonald's Angus burger.) Every time I've visited the Ōmakau calf sale, three-quarters of the cattle on offer are black Angus. I don't usually do what everyone else does, though, and I've been told that Shorthorns are often nice, quiet, attractive cattle that grow and marble well. Like with the Southdowns, I want to tip my hat to a breed that I like the look of, like the story of; a breed that's stood the test of time, a breed that's still commercially viable. I can't wait to start a little Shorthorn stud here at 'The Land' and hopefully help promote a breed that has arguably fallen on tougher times.

And there's more. You might remember that I figured out the hard way how you don't want to winter a heap of cattle without a tractor. But while I've got more cattle on the way and winter is coming, I still can't afford a new tractor. I can't afford an old one either. But I've got a plan.

In August last year, I was talking to a group of agricultural contractors at Te Pae in Christchurch and noticed a really engaged dude up in the

RAD

very front row. As tall as an All Black lock, old mate was on the edge of his seat, elbows resting on his long legs, large hands supporting his head. Totally engrossed. Most people are interested when I talk, but this bloke stood out. A week later, when I walked into the Tractor and Machinery Association Conference in Hamilton, the same guy was there. He soon introduced himself.

'G'day mate. Jaiden Drought. I heard you speak in Christchurch last week. You were brilliant.'

I thanked him, and apologised for him having to listen to me twice in the space of a week. Jaiden, who works for John Deere, had just been appointed president of the association. After I congratulated him, somehow we started talking about my previous winter when I'd fed out to nearly 30 cattle without a tractor and it had nearly broken me. I told Jaiden I had to either sell the majority of my cattle or buy a tractor, and I couldn't afford a tractor, plus I had to sell most of my cattle anyway to pay my tax.

The rest of the night went well, as these nights usually do. A nice graze, lots of laughter and a few tears. Then I got back in my rental, drove to Auckland and spent a few hours in the cot before being up at sparrow's fart to jump on a plane to Queenstown. I did a talk in Cromwell that morning then went and bought some lunch at my usual cafe, and when I left that cafe I noticed a text from an unknown number. 'Hi Matt, it's Jaiden Drought here from John Deere. I was speaking to you last night at the conference. I am interested in having a chat with you around your current tractor situation (I'm not trying to sell you one) and maybe a couple of options we could work through with you. If you get a chance, give me a bell, mate. Talk soon. Thanks.'

Was this bloke trying to hook me up with a tractor?

I rang him immediately and joked about him trying to sell me a tractor.

'Not at all, mate. I love what you do — I love your story-telling and I really think you're helping a lot of people and I think we should help you. I want to get you into one of our tractors, so you can run a few more cattle again, and also maybe talk to our people in New Zealand and Australia. Who knows where this could end up?'

I couldn't believe it, and told him that I wouldn't hold him to anything. If it happened, fantastic; if it didn't, no worries. But it gave me hope. After being away for a few days, the last leg of my journey through the Cromwell Gorge to home is always special and it was even more special that day. I was thinking about the Shorthorn cows that Fraser and I were talking about doing a deal on. I thought about how life might become just a little easier if I had a tractor.

Jaiden and I communicated over the next couple of months, and in the end John Deere and Otago Farm Machinery let me choose between two brand-new tractors — complete with bucket and forks to lift those big, heavy bales. I can't wait for that brand-new green-and-yellow tractor to turn up. In a lot of ways, I'm a very lucky man.

WHAT COMES NEXT?

I now know, probably as well as anyone, the importance of living in the present. This little farm and my family are helping me get better at living in the now. A meal together around the table. Kicking a ball around with the kids. Feeding the stock. Watching the sun going down on the farm. But when you're going through a rough spell, you need to consciously remind yourself why you're doing what you're doing and that you have things to look forward to.

I love watching the children grow. I notice changes when I'm away for just a few days. I'm looking forward to having even funnier and deeper conversations with my kids. I'm looking forward to watching them play more sport. To watching them find their way in the world. I'm looking forward to becoming even better friends with them, to helping them figure out what is actually really important. Because I'm away so much at the moment, every day at home feels special. I appreciate every meal. Every bed-time story. Every night that I get to lie down with my boys and make sure they go to sleep. I'm looking forward to having more time. More time with the family. More time on the water, in kayaks, on paddle-boards.

I'm looking forward to spending more time with Elle. Right now, we're like ships in the night; but that will change. I'm looking forward to travelling again, too. If we're ever lucky enough to be debt-free, at some point I want to lease out our house and our land and take the kids on a massive overseas trip. I don't want to take them to Disneyland or SeaWorld; I want to take them to Africa, Asia, South America. I want to show them what poverty looks like. I want to show them just how lucky they are calling Chatto Creek, Central Otago, New Zealand, home.

Here, I'm looking forward to breeding a few more Southdown sheep. To growing the size of my flock. I'm looking forward to more TV-free summer and autumn nights, cruising around my lambs saying to myself: 'Shit, 323/23 — she's really coming on.' I'm looking forward to seeing more of that golden glow when my animals are 'kissed' by the sun before it goes down behind the hills at the end of another day. I'm looking forward to breeding some full-blooded Swiss Valais Blacknose sheep — eventually — but I'm making sure I enjoy the breeding-up process along the way. I understand now that you can't wait to be happy — you have to be happy *now*, because now is all we've got.

Real, hard-working people who are doing their bit to produce good food for the world. There's not a whole lot more noble than that.

I'm looking forward to breeding a few Shorthorn cattle. And to placing bets with the kids on what colour and sex the calves will be. I'm looking forward to listening to my animals eat their tucker after allowing them to have some more of it. I'm looking forward to selling animals at sales, though I'm probably more excited about catching up with the people at those sales. Real, hard-working people who are doing their bit to produce good food for the world. There's not a whole lot more noble than that. I'm looking forward to eating phenomenal Southdown lamb, well-marbled Shorthorn beef and Berkshire pork. I'm looking forward to sitting around a big table and sharing that meat with family and friends. I'm looking forward to getting some chickens and to eating their eggs. I'm looking forward to turning Rock into a useful resource as well as a sweet pet.

I'm looking forward to the work involved in running this wee farm. To feeding out baleage in 'my' new John Deere tractor. And to topping my paddocks — I reckon I might even feel like a real farmer then. I'm looking forward to lamb-tailing — I'm going to turn that into a tradition. I'll invite some of my best friends in this world to come lamb-tailing at my place and we'll do a little bit of work, a lot of talking, a lot of laughing and a lot of partying. And hopefully they'll come back next year and every year after that. And I reckon we'll celebrate the fact that we're able to come back. We'll celebrate the fact that we're all still alive.

I'm definitely looking forward to life on the land becoming a little easier. I'm looking forward to putting in some more fences, some more irrigation, some yards. And lots of other things on the wish list.

I'm also looking forward to more helping, both me helping other people and other people helping me. Life's a whole lot easier with help. I couldn't live this life without my family, Elle, Bede, Finn and Bree. They're always helping me, even when they don't know they are. I couldn't farm here without Dennis and Christine's help and guidance. And all those good bastards — AP, OB, Adam, Robbo, Kyle, Dan, Willy, Scotty and Jared. I don't know if they'll ever know just how much they've helped me. It's not just helping me with seed, or feed, or irrigation, or shearing, or a helping hand; it's that they remind me that I'm actually worth helping. Then there's guys like Dave Robertson, Blair Robertson, Fraser Fletcher, and Jaiden Drought from John Deere: all of them have allowed me to be more than just a hobby farmer. I hope that's because they think I'm a decent bloke to have around; a bloke worth helping.

For my part, I'm looking forward to helping my people — the people who live around me, those in my community, rural New Zealanders, and just people in general. I'm so lucky. When I talk, people listen; and when people listen, you can have an impact on them — you can sway them, go some way towards influencing them one way or another. I now take that very seriously.

I'm also looking forward to just being. Looking forward to each day. My first cup of coffee in the morning. A piece of toast. Some banter with my kids. A laugh on the phone. A smile from a stranger. Tasting my food. The sun on my face. The view from the table. Kicks with the kids.

Away from the farm, there's so much we can do, so much to look forward to, without having to go far. Right now, I'm looking up at my in-laws' hill. There're rabbits up in them there hills, and I want to go up there with the kids and shoot some of those rabbits. Not because I enjoy killing — you know I don't — but rabbits are pests and there're too many of them up in them there hills. On top of that, it makes for a good adventure, and when you get up on top of those hills the views are amazing. I want to teach my kids about the importance of climbing to the top and enjoying the view. I want them to know that, sometimes, the view isn't as good as they'd thought it might be but that shouldn't stop them from climbing other hills or mountains. I want to learn how to fish, and once I've learnt how to fish I want to teach my kids how to fish.

I want to teach my kids about the importance of climbing to the top and enjoying the view.

Now that the kids are a little older, I want to do some more camping. I want to spend all day simply living. Sleep. Cook breakfast. Do some dishes. Explore the area you're camping in. Go fishing. Eat fresh fish for lunch. Do some dishes. Throw a Frisbee. Kick a football. Read a book. Meditate. Breathe. Cook some homegrown lamb or beef for dinner, with new potatoes, salad, mint. Talk about what we're grateful for over dinner. Do some dishes. Play cards with the kids. Sleep. I've actually been talking about buying kayaks and paddle-boards for a decade. Elle finally bought some the other day, and we're going to use them on these beautiful rivers and lakes that are all around us. We're going to put packs on our backs, and we're going to take the kids into the bush and we're going to walk. One foot after the other. We're going to marvel at the natural world we live

in. And when we're finished walking, we're going to cook and eat good, wholesome food. We're going to play some games with the kids, and then we're all going to go to sleep.

We're going to unplug from this chaotic world as often as we can. Get away from the news and the advertising and the messages that people send us no matter what day it is or what time of the day it is. We're going to be grateful, though, for every day; and when bad things happen, as they will, I'm going to try to tell myself that 'I'm not losing, I'm learning. I need this right now — this is all part of the plan.'

I'd love to turn 'The Land' into a full-time job. I'd love to build some accommodation and share our wee piece of paradise with others.

I'm now 47, and I'm not sure what I'm going to do when I grow up but I am looking forward to finding out. One thing is for certain, though: provided that we can continue to keep paying the bills, we're going to be farmers. Small-time farmers who take it really seriously because it's what we love, and when you love something you do it as much as you can. I'd love to turn 'The Land' into a full-time job. I'd love to build some accommodation and share our wee piece of paradise with others. Show off my heritage sheep and cattle and pigs, and the chickens we haven't got yet. Tell their story. Talk about how popular these breeds used to be, and how everyone got out of them as they chased efficiency and money. Maybe I'll share what I've learnt about how to live a better life. Who knows?

I've often thought about how much easier life would be if we moved into an ordinary house on a section. Never once, though, have I seriously considered doing that. In amongst all the death, blood, sweat and tears, there's so much beauty, so much joy, in living a wholesome life on the land. I reckon we're experiencing a greater sense of community and forging better, deeper connections. I'd like to think that life on the land won't always be this busy and this hard. I'd like to think that it'll get easier.

As time goes on, the children will be able to do more for themselves and will also be able to help more. Hopefully, I'll be able to put in more infrastructure to make life a little easier. Hopefully, I'll learn from my mistakes. I might just simplify what I'm trying to do here.

But if, for whatever reason, we can't hold on — let's say we can't pay the big mortgage, or we decide, in the end, that the costs of living this chaotic and brutal, yet beautiful, life outweigh the benefits — at least we know what it's like now. At least we will have made the most of the dash.

ACKNOWLEDGEMENTS

For me, writing is difficult because I don't have much time, I struggle to focus, and I don't like sitting down for long. So, I would never have been able to write this book if it hadn't been for my amazing wife, Elle, who would take our beautiful (yet often loud and chaotic) kids away from home for hours so that I could write. Elle must be really tired of parenting alone, and I'm extremely lucky to have her in my corner.

I'd also like to thank all my mates who were up for being photographed for the book, despite not knowing what I'd written about them in it.

Thanks to my brilliant editor, Teresa McIntyre, for what I like to call 'making honey out of dog shit'. Teresa took a pile of my words, polished them and put them in a sensible order when I didn't have the time or energy to do it. Thanks also to managing editor Leanne McGregor, designer Kate Barraclough, and proofreaders Mike Wagg and Tessa King.

To Lottie Hedley, thanks for capturing the beauty and the chaos of our little world here on The Land.

Finally, I'd like to thank Michelle Hurley and Allen & Unwin for asking me to write not one but two books. Without that I would never have had the confidence to write either. Many people have told me that my honesty has helped them, so I'm hugely grateful for the platform. Thank you.

THE LAND

First published in 2024

Allen & Unwin
Level 2, 10 College Hill, Freemans Bay
Auckland 1011, New Zealand
+64 (9) 377 3800
auckland@allenandunwin.com
www.allenandunwin.co.nz

83 Alexander Street
Crows Nest NSW 2065, Australia
+61 (2) 8425 0100

A catalogue record for this book is available from the National Library of New Zealand.

ISBN 978 1 99100 650 9

Design by Kate Barraclough
Set in Minion Pro and Brandon Text
Printed in China by 1010 Printing Limited

1 3 5 7 9 10 8 6 4 2

FSC
www.fsc.org
MIX
Paper | Supporting responsible forestry
FSC® C016973